NATIVE
AMERICAN

myths

NATIVE
AMERICAN

myths

Steve Eddy

TEACH YOURSELF BOOKS

For UK order queries: please contact Bookpoint Ltd, 130 Milton Park, Abingdon, Oxon OX14 4SB. Telephone: (44) 01235 827720. Fax: (44) 01235 400454. Lines are open 9.00–18.00, Monday to Saturday, with a 24-hour message answering service. Email address: orders@bookpoint.co.uk

For U.S.A. order queries: please contact McGraw-Hill Customer Services, P.O. Box 545, Blacklick, OH 43004-0545, U.S.A. Telephone: 1-800-722-4726. Fax: 1-614-755-5645.

For Canada order queries: please contact McGraw-Hill Ryerson Ltd., 300 Water St, Whitby, Ontario L1N 9B6, Canada. Telephone: 905 430 5000. Fax: 905 430 5020.

Long renowned as the authoritative source for self-guided learning – with more than 30 million copies sold worldwide – the *Teach Yourself* series includes over 300 titles in the fields of languages, crafts, hobbies, business and education.

British Library Cataloguing in Publication Data
A catalogue record for this title is available from The British Library.

Library of Congress Catalog Card Number: On file

First published in UK 2001 by Hodder Headline Plc, 338 Euston Road, London, NW1 3BH.

First published in US 2001 by Contemporary Books, A Division of The McGraw-Hill Companies, 4255 West Touhy Avenue, Lincolnwood (Chicago), Illinois 60712–1975 U.S.A.

The 'Teach Yourself' name and logo are registered trade marks of Hodder & Stoughton Ltd.

Typeset by Transet Limited, Coventry, England.
Printed in Great Britain for Hodder & Stoughton Educational, a division of Hodder Headline Plc, 338 Euston Road, London NW1 3BH by Cox & Wyman Ltd, Reading, Berkshire.

Impression number   10 9 8 7 6 5 4 3 2 1
Year   2007 2006 2005 2004 2003 2002 2001

CONTENTS

THE LAND OF THE DEAD

INTRODUCTION

A vital factor in the development of the human race has been its use of symbols to represent ideas or urges that cannot easily be defined. A symbol can magically bring an idea to life by appealing to the creative power of the imagination. It can also offer several layers of meaning in a single image. For example when Theseus tracks down the Minotaur in the Cretan labyrinth, he lays down a thread to guide his return. This may symbolize divine inspiration, or the link between the conscious mind and the unconscious. The labyrinth itself can be seen as a symbol of the individual's tortuous journey to self-knowledge and of the mysteries of the feminine.

Myths, then, are symbolic stories. They have evolved through oral tradition and they have guided, inspired and psychically nourished humanity for thousands of years.

Myths interpreted

Mythology has been used by poets, playwrights and artists for centuries. The nineteenth century, however, saw the rise of scientific rationalism and of social realism in the arts. Myths were in danger of being demoted to the status of quaint old stories about non-existent gods. A 'myth' began to mean simply a widely held but mistaken belief.

With the rise of psychology, however, myths found a new status – although there was controversy about their origins and functions. Freud saw them as expressing repressed impulses commonly found in the personal unconscious. For example the myth of Oedipus expressed a boy's socially unacceptable desire to kill his father and sleep with his mother.

Claude Levi-Strauss saw myths as stemming from a human need to make sense of the world. By this model, the myths worldwide in which human beings are fashioned from clay by a divine potter, such as the Egyptian Ptah, fulfil our need to know how and why we came to be here. Other widespread myths explain death and the seasons.

Another view focuses on myth as magic. Stories of hero gods descending into the Underworld in the west and emerging in the east, reflect the setting and rising of the sun. Myths in which an ageing goddess is reborn as a youthful virgin reflect the return of spring after winter. This kind of myth must have reassured early man. More important, it is likely that the repeated telling of stories symbolizing the rising of the sun, the return of spring or the ripening of crops was a magical way of making these things happen.

Many commentators have noted the similarities between myths in different cultures. One theory is that this can be explained by migration, trade contact and the exchange of myths between conquerors and conquered. There is certainly some truth in this, for example in the interweaving of Aztec and Mayan myths. However, this can hardly explain similarities such as the appearance of 'trickster' gods: the infant Hermes stealing Apollo's cattle, the Norse Loki cutting off the golden tresses of Thor's wife Sif or a similarly mischievous deity of the North American Winnebago Indians.

Jung and the theory of archetypes

The exploration of myths found a new dimension in the work of Carl Jung. Whereas Freud saw the unconscious as being entirely personal, the product of a lifetime's repressed sexual urges, Jung identified a layer of consciousness below this – the collective unconscious. This is a vast psychic pool of energized symbols shared by humanity as a whole. It is filled with 'archetypes': symbolic figures, such as the trickster just mentioned, the mother, and the father. They also include the animus and anima, which are the undeveloped and largely unacknowledged opposite sex parts of, respectively, the female and male psyche. Another important archetype is the shadow, which embodies all that we deny in ourselves and 'project' onto people we dislike. These archetypes form the *dramatis personae* of myth. Thus myths offer a way for cultures to explore their collective impulses and to express them creatively, rather than harmfully.

Myths, dreams and the individual

Jung recognized dreams as doorways between an individual and the collective unconscious. Many dreams, he said, expressed archetypes that might otherwise be projected onto the waking world as irrational fears, delusions or hatreds. Joseph Campbell, who has developed this idea, writes, 'Here we can begin to see a way of working with myths on a personal level, for our own development.' Campbell and other writers have also pointed out that myths are still emerging and developing in the present day. On the social level we see this in the recurrence of mythical archetypes in popular culture, for example in the hugely successful *Star Wars* films.

Jung saw myths as representing the individual's journey towards psychic wholeness. The aim of this book is not only to show the power of myth to entertain and enrich on a narrative level, but also to facilitate this journey. It retells the myths and explores the interpretations – cultural, moral psychological and spiritual – to which they lend themselves. It also shows how the themes of Native American myths echo those of other cultures worldwide, in a way that argues a fundamental psychic content common to all humanity.

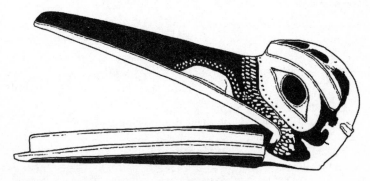

Ceremonial bird mask (North-West)

1 | INTRODUCTION TO NATIVE AMERICAN MYTHS

Prior to European colonization, Native American culture was non-literate and intensely tribal. It was often socially sophisticated, yet its technology was stone age. Nowadays Native Americans read and write and have to varying degrees adopted the European-based lifestyle of the new Americans. However, the oral storytelling tradition is still strong and in places the recounting of myths plays a vital part in religious ceremonies. Moreover, while intertribal hostilities are now limited to occasional legal disputes over land, tribal identities are still very strong. These are reflected in the myths and stories presented in this volume. At the same time they contain many shared themes.

Myth, legends and folktales

Many of the stories in this volume could as well be called 'folktales' as myths. However, in Europe the folktale is usually thought of as being on a lower level than the myth. This may be true of some Native American folktales, but certainly not all. The key to understanding their status lies in the spiritual outlook of the tellers. If there is a useful distinction to be made between myths and folktales, it is that myths have a religious content and folktales deal with something humbler. However, insofar as it is possible to generalize about several hundred distinct tribes, the Native American attitude towards the universe is that everything is animated by divinity. There is little of the European distinction between the sacred and the profane.

Hence many of the myths in this volume appear to be about ordinary people. In many cases these people are not even named or they are known by a convenient tag, such as Rabbit Boy – who was brought up by rabbits. Neither is there much attempt to characterize them, since they stand for universal principles which are considered to be more important than individual traits. A story may reflect the character of the original shaman whose vision or dream first generated it; it will certainly reflect the character of the tribe; but most of all it will express something deeply rooted in the collective unconscious.

It should also be noted that whereas Greek myths were shaped and ordered by classical authors, few Native American myths were written down before the late nineteenth century. Thus the apparent contradictions and inconsistencies of the right-brain oral tradition are still very much present. They do not always follow the European pattern of dramatic tension leading to resolution, with loose ends neatly tied up, and characters sometimes drift out of a story once they have served their purpose.

Native American spirituality

A wide range of religious beliefs exists among Native American tribes. As noted earlier, some belief systems involve pantheons of gods and spirits, and these are probably most developed among tribes in the South-West. However, among all tribes there is a strong sense that behind all individual spirits and personifications of the divine, there is a single creative life-force, sometimes called 'the Great Mystery', which expresses itself throughout the universe, in every human, animal, tree and grain of sand. Every story, too, is a working out of this life-force.

The role of animals

An aspect of this outlook is the major role played in the stories by animals, who often speak to humans and assist them. Most tribes thought of individual members of a species as expressions of the spiritual archetype of that species, which in turn embodied a particular spirit power. The bear, for example, was often associated with healing (see 'The Medicine Grizzly Bear', Chapter 12). This attitude reflects a closeness to the natural world. In a Greek myth the archetypal role of helper to a hero is played by a human or a god; in Native American myths the helper is usually an animal.

The Four Directions

Another key feature of the Native American spiritual outlook is found in the powers ascribed to the Four Directions, which occur either literally or in symbolic form throughout the stories. These are often represented by particular colours or by animals. They are often linked with the four winds or with the daily cycle of the sun. The following table below compares the Navajo and Lakota directional associations.

	Navajo	Lakota
East	Red (dawn)	Yellow
South	Blue (noon)	White
West	Yellow (evening)	Black
North	Black (north)	Red

These systems are similar to the Four Elements in the Western tradition. The Four Directions can also be tentatively related to Jung's four functions: thought, intuition, feeling and sensation.

The Four Directions have to be in balance for all to be well with the world, and often a central point of balance is identified as a fifth direction; for example, four brothers represent the outer directions and their sister the centre. In addition one often finds the idea that the world must be balanced in terms of light–dark, male–female or sun–moon. This may relate to the Asian origins of Native American peoples, and it seems appropriate to refer to these polarities by the Chinese terms: *yin* (passive) and *yang* (active).

Narrative types

Creation myths

One major category of Native American myth recounts the beginning of the world. Many of these myths, especially those of the South-West, involve an emergence from consecutive worlds. This may relate to the evolution of the human mind to present-day consciousness. These myths also contain a powerful sense of the universe gradually being ordered and balanced, often in terms of the forces just discussed. These emergence myths are often attached to a flood myth, so that humans emerge from a flooded world or into a flooded world which must then be drained for habitation.

Hero myths

Another common type of myth is that of the hero. The hero may be divine, as in the case of Glooskap (see Chapter 15) or the Navajo Hero Twins (see Chapter 16). He may be born in extraordinary circumstances and possess unusual powers, like Rabbit Boy (Chapter 10) or may even be an ordinary young man who achieves something great through personal endeavour and the grace of animal-spirit helpers. Frequently this type of hero comes from humble origins. However, in Native American myths more than in those of any other culture, the heroic act must benefit the people. It is not enough to be a great warrior or kill monsters: the tribe comes before personal glory. Moreover, spiritual power may be more important than physical courage. Similarly, it is of greater value to bring back an important ritual to the tribe than to kill enemies.

Typically the hero goes on a quest or takes up a challenge. There is frequently a strong element of initiation in the story. This often involves the hero separating from the mother, seeking out the father (or father-figure), overcoming the father's anger and rejection, and being given gifts which signify acceptance.

Not all hero myths, however, fit this pattern. The divine hero, such as Glooskap, is already an initiate and may not have to be tested (although the tale we have may be a fragment of one which originally contained testing). His role is to set an example and to save the people from a threat. This threat is often some form of life-denying monster or ogre. Psychologically this monster represents the ego (the socially conditioned sense of self, as apart from the rest of the world), in its life-denying aspect. The ego becomes life-denying when an individual identifies with possessions and self-image. Psychic energy is diverted towards a bolstering of the ego at the expense of a living connection with the divine.

The Trickster

An important category of tales focuses on the trickster archetype. There are tricksters in myth worldwide, such as Loki, mentioned in the Introduction. However, Native American culture is particularly rich in them. Notable examples are Coyote and Iktome. The trickster is an ambiguous figure who demonstrates the qualities of early human development (both cultural and psychological) that make civilization possible and yet which cause problems: rebelliousness, a desire for improvement, the will and ability to deceive and, of course, curiosity. He is an expression of the least developed stage of life, which is dominated by physical appetites. His preoccupation is with gratifying his own needs.

However, the trickster is full of vitality, can be charismatic, and is ingenious – even if his cleverness often gets him into trouble. He has been described, in Jungian terms, as the hero's Shadow. In fact, wherever there is a hero, a trickster of some sort is likely to be close at hand.

Tales of the afterlife

Among Native Americans there is a widespread belief in reincarnation and this is often expressed in the myths. Often there is a belief that pure souls will go on to a spirit world, but that those who still need to develop will return to this one. An example of this type of myth is found in the story of Sapana (Chapter 14). The other view of the afterlife found in the myths is of a land of the dead irrevocably cut off from this world. This is found in the 'Orphic' tale of 'The loving husband' (Chapter 20).

Tribes represented in this guide

The myths and tales in this guide have been selected to give a cross-section of the most important types and themes. It would be impossible in a work of this size to cover more than a small number of tribes. Those covered are now briefly outlined.

Algonquin

These members of the Algonquian language group originally lived in what is now Quebec province in Canada. As a result of their alliance with the French, they became sworn enemies of the Iroquois, at whose hands they suffered heavy defeats.

Apache

The Apache originally came from the far North-West, and the Apachean languages are related to other Athabascan languages spoken in Canada. They did not reach the South-West until the start of the second millennium. As late as 1700 there were Plains Apache farmers in Kansas, but the introduction of the horse enabled the Comanche and Ute to push them south and west. The Jicarilla Apache relied more on agriculture than did other branches of the tribe and were less warlike.

Arapaho

These members of the Algonquian language group migrated from what is now Minnesota to the plains between the Yellowstone River and the Rio Grande. They were allies of the Cheyenne, but were friendly towards European settlers. Culturally they had much in common with the Lakota, including their version of the Sundance.

Blackfoot

The Blackfoot are Algonquian language speakers. They were tipi-dwelling nomads of the Northern Plains. In the eighteenth century they drifted into the Montana area hunting buffalo. They were feared by other groups and were often at war with the Cree, Lakota and Crow.

Caddo

The Caddo, members of the Caddoan language group, were highly successful farmers living in what is now Texas (which takes its name from a Caddo word for their confederacy of tribal groups). Their relative wealth and density of population led them to develop complex social institutions. They lived in grass huts.

Cheyenne

The Cheyenne are members of the Algonquian linguistic family. They were farmers, hunters and gatherers in central Minnesota, but were driven west by the Lakota and Ojibway in the seventeenth century. They became firm allies of the Lakota and fought alongside them at the Battle of the Little Bighorn.

Lakota

A powerful nation of the Siouan language group. The insulting term by which their enemies the Ojibway referred to them was rendered into French as Nadouessioux. From this came the common name, Sioux. However, these people usually call themselves the Lakota, which is the name of their largest dialect group, the others being the Dakota and Nakota. The Lakota once lived in the woodlands of present-day Minnesota, but migrated west to avoid the Ojibway. On the Plains they became great hunters of buffalo, as well as the last tribe to hold out against the US government. The last battles were fought over white incursions into the Black Hills, which were sacred to the Lakota and had been promised to them for ever.

Navajo

The Navajo are the largest group in modern-day USA. Like the related Apache, they were latecomers to the South-West who migrated from the far North-West. They speak an Apachean language which is one of the Athabascan family. They probably moved south in around 1000 CE, since when they have been strongly influenced culturally and in their myths by neighbouring Pueblo tribes, including the Hopi.

Pawnee

Members of the Caddoan language family. The Pawnee inhabited what is now Nebraska. They often engaged in warfare with neighbours, especially their principal enemy, the Lakota. They were farmers and lived in earth lodges in small villages. Animal spirits played a particularly important role in their religion.

Seneca

This tribe of the Iroquoian linguistic group inhabited what is now New York state and Ohio. They were one of the most important members of the five nations originally comprising the Iroquois League. They lived by farming, hunting and fishing.

Zuni

The Zuni form a distinct linguistic family. In appearance, culture and social organization they resemble other sedentary Pueblo peoples such as the Hopi. They are farmers, also noted for weaving and pottery. Their complex religious rituals were presided over by a powerful priestly caste.
afterlife 5, 117–21

Bird head totem pole detail (North-West)

2 | THE LAKOTA CREATION

This account of creation according to the Lakota (Sioux) tribe is based on that collected by James R. Walker. It shows a process of creation giving rise to a hierarchy of gods. Though individually identified, they are all manifestations of the one spirit, Wakan Tanka.

In the time when there was no time and no distinct thing, there was Inyan and his spirit was Wakan Tanka, the Great Mystery. There was also Han, but she was only the black of darkness. Inyan was shapeless and soft, but his blue blood contained mighty powers. Now Inyan began to long for another being so that he could exercise his powers upon it. He knew that to do so he would have to use his own blood and that however much blood he used, that much power he would lose. So he decided to create a being that was still a part of himself, in order to retain his power. He created a great disc spreading over and around himself to where there is no beyond, and this disc he called Maka, Mother Earth.

In creating Maka, Inyan opened his veins and sacrificed his blood, which became the waters. His own body shrivelled up, becoming hard but powerless. Water cannot contain power and so the power separated out, some of it becoming the blue dome of the great sky spirit, Skan, whose edge adjoined the edge of Earth Mother Maka.

Maka, however, was dissatisfied because Inyan had not made her as a completely separate being. Moreover, she was cold and naked, and she demanded that Inyan banish Han, the darkness. When Inyan protested that he no longer had the power to do this, she taunted him with his impotence, until he agreed to appeal to Skan. This is how Skan, Ruler of the Sky, became the supreme judge of all things. Skan ruled that Maka had to remain a part of Inyan, but to appease her he made Anp, the red light and banished the darkness of Han to the Underworld.

Now there was light everywhere, but this was still not good enough for Maka, for there was no warmth and no shade. So Skan took something from Inyan and from Maka, and from himself and made Wi, the brilliant disc of the sun, whose spirit was Wi-akan. Wi shone on the world and everything became hot and bright.

Maka was still not happy, for now there was no respite from the burning heat. So Skan directed Anp and Han – the red light and the darkness – to follow one another, each remaining for a time upon the earth, and he ordered the great sun Wi to go before Anp to the Underworld and follow him above the world. Now there was daytime and night-time, and Earth Mother Maka was at last satisfied.

The gods enjoyed their feasts in the Underworld, and it was here, too, that Skan created human beings, the Pte, as their servants. The chief of the humans was Wa, whose wife Ka bore a beautiful daughter, Ite. The Wind God Tate made her his wife and she gave him sons. Unfortunately, Ite was very vain and so Inyan's son Ksa, the God of Wisdom, plotted with the enticing and deceitful demon Gnaksi to make her usurp the place of the Moon Goddess Hanwi as wife of bright-shining Wi.

Ite's mother Ka was a seer and she foretold that if Ite sat with Wi, then Ite and her parents would live for ever. For this reason, Ka and her husband Wa were more than happy to collude in the plot hatched by Ksa and the trickster Gnaski.

Accordingly, at the next feast of the gods, Ite sat in Hanwi's place and Wi fell in love with her. Hanwi hid her face in shame and Ite's husband Tate was full of grief. But Skan, with his all-seeing sky-eye, saw this and pronounced sentence on Ite: for her crime, her unborn son would leave her and she would for ever after have two faces, one beautiful and one horrifyingly ugly. She would become Anog Ite, Two-Faced Woman.

Skan ruled that, for their part in the plot, Wa and Ka would live forever separate, as a wizard and a witch. Ksa, for misusing his intelligence, he condemned to a life as an outcast, whose wisdom would become mere cunning and who would become trapped by his own mischievous scheming. He would henceforth be known as Iktome, the Trickster. Finally, Skan decreed that bright-shining Wi, for his weakness, would no longer have Hanwi for a wife. To compensate Hanwi, Skan gave her a time of the month that was her own, the time between the new and full moon.

COMMENTARY

This myth attempts to explain the origins of the universe from first principles. It contains seasonal elements, but it is also a metaphor for humanity's spiritual evolution. A major theme is that of self-sacrifice.

Inyan

Inyan is a first manifestation of Wakan Tanka, the Great Mystery or Great Power, who is pure spirit. The name Inyan (or Iyan) means 'Stone', but before the creation of Maka, Inyan is soft and shapeless. At this point then he is merely undifferentiated matter. The distinction between Wakan Tanka and this primal manifestation is reflected in some other Native American creation myths, such as that of the Hopi. Even in Inyan, spirit has partially descended into something like a physical form, although this form has yet to descend from the indivisible 'One' to the myriad forms that make up the universe.

To the Lakota, the key factor is Inyan's self-sacrifice in giving his lifeblood to make the universe. The idea that spirit makes a sacrifice by descending into matter is found in many belief systems, including Christianity. However, it is particularly strong in Lakota culture. In the Lakota Sundance, young men have cherrywood skewers driven through their chests and then dance round a cottonwood tree to which the skewers are attached by thongs. Participants must continually blow on their eagle-bone whistles (representing the sun), and pull back on the thongs, until eventually they break free. This dance symbolizes human connection to the world axis, and to the sun, and it is performed as an act of self-sacrifice for the tribe or for someone in need. But it is also a means of repaying spirit for the original sacrifice in becoming matter.

In the version of the myth given here, Inyan creates Maka so that he will have something over which to exercise his powers. A slightly different version describes him as wanting to exercise his compassion. Not all creation myths ascribe a motive to the creator in this way. Doing so suggests a sophisticated attempt to 'see into the mind of god'.

Maka – Mother Earth

In Maka we begin to see a slightly less abstract personage. Inyan makes her as an extension of himself, and her desire to become separate suggests a drive for physical manifestation to become detached from the spirit. Skan's ruling that she must remain part of Inyan relates, on the mundane level, to stone (Inyan) and earth (Maka) being inseparable. On a deeper level this points to the continuing connection between spirit and matter.

Maka's continual complaints about her condition, and her taunting of Inyan, express the process by which the universe has evolved – through conflict. Philosophically this is related to the Chinese concept of yin and yang, opposites whose duality sets up an ever shifting dynamic. In another kind of creation myth, that of emergence (seen in the next chapter), humanity's ejection from each world in turn is always caused by some form of conflict. In the Lakota myth, the conflict is inherent in the human condition: it is between the ideal and the reality.

Skan

The second phase of creation, and of descent from spirit, is represented by Skan. He relates to the same stage of human evolution that in Greek myth is portrayed by the forcible separation of Ouranos (the sky) and Gaia (the earth). This shows a shift from the unconscious state of blissful union with the divine, to the conscious state of separation from it. However, this separation also brings discrimination, which is why Skan, like that other sky god Zeus, becomes a judge. Perhaps this is why it falls to Skan to create human beings.

The birth of a pantheon

As with many creation myths, such as the Greek, Indian and Polynesian, there is a gradual move towards diversification and fragmentation of the original life-force. Gods begin to represent different human drives, or parts of the psyche, as well as natural forces. Thus we see Ksa as God of Wisdom (later degraded to mere cunning) and Tate as the Wind God. The humans are semi-divine, in that they are able to feast with the gods, and Wi, the Sun God, is even prepared to leave his wife for the beautiful Ite. Ite's vanity resembles that of Aphrodite and creates conflict in a similar way. As 'Two-Faced Woman' she also represents summer and winter.

Typically, as the gods diversify they argue, just as there are warring factions within the human psyche. We also see in this myth, as the source of their argument, the familiar theme of humans seeking immortality, while the punishment of Wa and Ka may reflect the polarizing of the sexes.

3 | **THE EMERGENCE INTO THE FOURTH WORLD**

Many creation myths describe an emergence from beneath this world. The following Jicarilla Apache myth is adapted from nineteenth-century sources.

At the beginning of time there was nothing on this earth. It was a dark, desolate place, with high winds lashing an endless ocean. Only the Haktins, the gods, lived here and all creatures lived in an Underworld beneath the water. It was dark there and so human beings, and the animals that now love the sun, wanted more light; but the creatures of the night wanted to keep the darkness. So the creatures – who in those days all spoke the same language – argued about this, until in the end they agreed to settle the dispute by playing the 'thimble and button game'.

In dim firelight the people and animals drew closer to begin their contest. The sharp-eyed birds of the day were able to see where the button was and so the people and day animals won the first round. At this, the morning star began to shine and the black bear fled into the darkness. The people also won the second round, at which the sky grew light in the east and the brown bear also lumbered away. A third time, it grew brighter, and the puma padded off, growling. They played a fourth game, which the people also won, and the sun rose fully, while the night owl swooped off into a hollow tree.

It was light now, but the people were still underground, so when the sun spied another world through a hole in the roof, they all wanted to go there. Now the Haktins wanted to help them and it was they who had all the materials for making worlds. So White Haktin, Black Haktin, Holy Boy and Red Boy brought sand of different colours, and built it up into four mounds for the people.

They brought a black clay bowl filled with water to help things to grow. Then they began to sing their song of creation.

Hearing the song, the people began to plant out the four mounds. On the eastern mound they planted bushes that would bear black fruit; in the south they planted bushes that would bear blue fruit; in the west the fruits were to be yellow and in the north there were to be fruits of many colours. In time the mounds grew into mountains and the bushes blossomed and became heavy with ripe fruit.

One day two girls climbed up to pick fruit and flowers and this made the mountains stop growing. The people sent the great wind Cyclone to find the girls, but the mountains still refused to grow. This was a problem, because the mountains were not yet high enough for the people to get into the other world. They made ladders of feathers, but these were too weak. Then four buffalo offered their horns as ladder rungs and at last the people could climb out of the Underworld – although the buffalo horns have been bent ever since.

Finding themselves in the outer world, the people tethered the sun and moon with spider threads and sent them aloft to give light. The earth was, of course, still underwater, but now four storms began to roll the waters away: a black storm blew to the east, a blue to the south, a yellow one to the west, and a many-coloured storm to the north. It still required someone to discover whether the land was safe to walk on, and so the polecat went out – only to find that the earth was too soft: his legs sank and turned black. The same thing happened to the badger. Then the beaver went out and began to build dams to save what was left of the water. Finally, the grey crow went out, but became preoccupied with feasting on dead fish and frogs. The people punished him by turning him black.

Now the earth was dry except for the lakes, rivers and sea. The people emerged from the hole and travelled east, then south, then west and then north, each time stopping at the ocean. Tribes stopped wherever they wanted, but the Jicarilla kept on circling the emergence hole, until the Creator became angry. 'Where do you want to stop?' he demanded and they told him: 'At the centre of the earth.' And that is where they live to this day.

COMMENTARY

This is one of many 'emergence' or 'gestation' myths worldwide in which the earth gives birth to itself. It is like a womb containing the seed that will eventually grow into the world that we know. In fact, the seed image is reinforced by the fact that the Haktins (gods or spirits) regard water as necessary even to make the mountains themselves grow, although water here also represents 'the water of life', a medium by which the life-force is able to distribute itself.

Some south-western tribes have a more complex emergence myth, in which human beings emerge from a succession of worlds, as if gradually working their way out of a series of Chinese boxes. In both the Navajo creation myth (see Chapter 4) and the Hopi equivalent the current world is the fourth. The Jicarilla myth contains a hint of this sense of progressive evolution in the four games that the creatures play and in the ladder by which they climb out of the lower world. The Navajo 'Holy Ones', with their characteristic colours, are similar to the Haktins.

The starting point for the myth is a dark world covered with water. In a sense the world beneath the water is one of potential. This resembles the state of affairs in the Genesis myth, when 'the earth was without form and void, and darkness was upon the face of the deep'. In Genesis, too (as in the Lakota creation myth), the creation of light is a priority. In the Jicarilla myth light comes into being as a result of a competition between the concepts of light and dark. Interestingly it is a feature of the more complex emergence myths that each successive emergence is the result of conflict. The game played by the day and night creatures is a mild version of this – although the fact that they all speak the same language shows that they are still spiritually connected. It is significant that full daylight is preceded by the Morning Star (Venus), who to the Apache is an important spirit and a bringer of culture.

Significantly, too, it is the sun who first glimpses the world above. The sun is most often associated with the male principle and with heroic individuation from the womb of the mother. This suggests the evolution of consciousness from oneness with nature, to self-awareness; from the watery darkness of the unconscious, to ego awareness.

A key feature of the myth is the placing of the four mounds of sand by the Haktins. These represent the Four Directions, which are of huge importance in Native American belief (see Chapter 1). The four colours of the fruits are those which the Apache associate with each of the directions: black (east); blue (south); yellow (west); and multi-coloured (north). Thus the new world is properly balanced, standing on its four pillars. The emphasis on planting reflects the fact that the Jicarilla were a relatively peaceful branch of the Apache, with a well-developed system of agriculture. The planting therefore represents part of their cultural evolution.

However, the Jicarilla also adopted the buffalo hunting of the Plains tribes and the buffalo-horn ladder refers to this. Intrinsic to this hunting culture were respect and gratitude for the animal that gave itself up to the hunter. Hence there is a Lakota emergence myth in which the tribe emerge from a cave in the Black Hills, tempted by promises of an easy life on the surface. When they find that in fact life is hard, their holy man Tatanka generously turns himself into a buffalo in order to feed them. In the Jicarilla myth the buffalo provides his horns; this willingness to make a personal sacrifice for the sake of the tribe is also a factor in cultural evolution.

As with some other Native American myths, such as 'The Monster Boys and the Flood' (Chapter 6), emergence is combined with the deluge. The watery world into which the Jicarilla emerge resembles both the primal world of Genesis and the world of Noah. Myths of a great flood are found all over the world and there is some evidence that they have a historical basis. However, the subsidence of the flood also represents the emergence of consciousness and self-awareness. The sending out of animals to check the water level is reminiscent of Noah (who sends out a dove) and also makes animals the predecessors of humans on the new world. The explanations of how the polecat and badger got black legs, and why the crow is black, while obviously rationalizations, perhaps demonstrate the understanding of cause and effect, and the knowledge of good and bad, that became possible once human beings had become self-conscious.

The circling of the emergence hole, which resembles that of the Hopi, probably stems from actual migrations when the Apache arrived in the South-West. The final settling in one place may refer to the Apaches' move from the nomadic hunter-gatherer existence to one which was based at least partly on agriculture.

4 | THE CREATION OF FIRST MAN AND FIRST WOMAN

This account of the Navajo creation is based partly on a report by Washington Matthews in 1897, partly on Leland C. Wyman's *Blessingway*, but also on a number of other sources. The account here follows Matthews in having First Man and First Woman created by the gods in the fourth world but in some accounts they have existed in previous worlds.

The first people to inhabit the earth were only partly human. They took the form of animals, insects or masked spirits. They emerged from each of three successive worlds. Although in each world things began well, after a while the people began to fight among themselves and to commit adultery, until the time came when they were banished by the gods and had to leave that world behind and move into the next. They had been well received by the Swallow People in the second world, but had to struggle with the Cat People, who were tricksters. Driven up to the third world, they met the evil Snake People.

Finally they emerged on this earth, known as the 'Glittering World', by climbing up inside a magical hollow reed. In previous worlds they had found no other people like themselves, but in the fourth world they emerged to find that the Pueblo people had already arrived.

The very first world had been dark and barren, but this fourth world was a mixture of dark and light and the sky was black and blue. No sun, moon or stars shone yet, but there were four snow-covered peaks standing like sentinels on the horizon in each of the directions. The gods had thought carefully about where to put these sacred mountains and they began placing all the stars with similar care. But the trickster Coyote became impatient and shook a corner of the blanket on which the stars were laid out, so that they flew up like sparks from a fire and stayed wherever they happened to land in the sky.

Once in the Glittering World, the people built a sweatlodge of branches and hides in order to purify themselves, and they sang the Blessing Song. They built a hogan in which to live, constructing it exactly as Talking God had instructed them, as a mirror of the universe in which they found themselves. In this hogan they began to arrange and order their world, naming the four sacred mountains surrounding their territory, each with its sacred stone. The peak to the east they named White Shell Mountain; the one to the south became Turquoise Mountain; to the west, Abalone Shell Mountain; and to the north, Big Sheep Mountain.

In the first autumn after emerging into this world, the people heard the distant sound of a great, booming voice calling from where the sun rises in the east. They stopped what they were doing and listened attentively. Soon they heard the voice again, this time louder than before. Again they listened and it was louder still. In a moment four mysterious beings appeared. These were the Holy Ones: Black Body, the God of Fire; Blue Body, the sprinkler; Yellow Body, the God of Water; and White Body, the God of this World.

Using sign language, the Holy Ones tried to teach the people, but without success, because the people could not understand the signs. When the deities had gone, the people talked excitedly among themselves, trying to reach an agreement on what the signs had meant. The gods appeared on four consecutive days, each time trying to teach the people, but always with the same result.

On the fourth day, Black Body stayed behind when the other gods had gone, and spoke to the people in their own language: 'Since you do not understand our signs, I will explain to you what we mean. We want to create a people who look more like us. True, your bodies resemble ours, but you have the teeth, feet and claws of beasts and insects. Our new humans will have hands and feet like ours. Also, you are dirty and your smell is offensive. We will return in twelve days' time. Make sure that you are clean then.'

The twelfth day came and the people had washed themselves thoroughly. Then they dried their skin with cornmeal – yellow for the women and white for the men. Soon they heard the familiar distant call of the approaching gods. It sounded four times, each time louder and closer. When the gods appeared, Blue Body and Black Body were each carrying a sacred buckskin. White Body carried two ears of corn, one yellow, one white, each heavy with grains.

The gods spread one buckskin out on the ground with the head to the west. On this they placed the two ears of corn with their sprouting tips to the east. Under the white ear they placed a white eagle's feather and under the yellow a yellow eagle's feather. They laid the second buckskin on top with its head to the east. Then they told the people to stand back so that the wind could enter. From the east and the west, the white and yellow winds blew between the buckskins. And as the wind blew, the eight gods, the Mirage People, came and walked around the objects on the ground four times. While they did this, the tips of the eagle feathers moved. When the Mirage People had finished, the top buckskin was lifted. To the astonishment of the watching people, the ears of corn had gone and in their place were two godlike human beings, opening their eyes with wonder for the first time. The white ear had become First Man, the yellow ear First Woman, and the Holy Wind had breathed into them, filling them with the breath of life.

The gods now instructed the people to build a brushwood enclosure for First Man and First Woman, and the couple entered it. The gods told them: 'Now you will live together as husband and wife.'

After only four days, First Woman bore twins who were neither male nor female. In another four days she gave birth to a boy and a girl, who grew up in four days and began to live together as husband and wife. First Man and First Woman had five pairs of twins and all except the first became couples who had children.

Four days after the last twins were born, the gods returned and took First Man and First Woman away to the eastern mountain, where the gods have their home. The couple stayed there for four days, and then all their children were taken there for four days to be instructed in the ways of the gods.

Now that they had been instructed by the gods, the brothers and sisters separated. They kept their first marriages secret and married the Mirage People. They also kept secret the mysteries they had learned from the gods. And since a new generation was born every four days and grew up in the same length of time, the children of First Man and First Woman quickly populated the land.

COMMENTARY

The Navajo have a particularly rich system of myths, which they share in part both with their relations the Apache and with Pueblo tribes (including the Hopi) that were already living in the South-West when the Navajo migrated there. The Navajo learned the arts of pottery and agriculture from the Pueblos, as well as the sand painting for which they have become famous. Their mythical concept of an emergence through a succession of four worlds is shared with the Hopi, although the Hopi see this current world as only the fourth in a series of seven.

The expression of Navajo spirituality

As Donald Sandner says in his *Navajo Symbols of Healing*: 'The Navajo world is thick with deity. Every natural force, every geographical feature, every plant, animal, or meteorological phenomenon has its supernatural power.' The deities, such as the four Holy People and the eight Mirage People who appear in the account given here, are the main initiators of action and development in the myths. Their power is honoured and perpetuated in the world by the enaction of the myths in a complex interrelated body of rituals known as 'Chant Ways'. Again, as Sandner says: 'The myths by themselves have no substance unless they are embedded in the ritual action of the chants.'

The fullest enactment of the creation myth, of which the story of First Man and First Woman is a part, is contained in the Blessingway, which is a ceremony that continues for several days. The Navajo, like the Hopi, consider singing, or chanting, vital to the process of creation and healing. Other Navajo Chant Ways are used, along with disposable dry paintings made of sand, pollen and petals, to cure illness or to tackle a particular problem. Blessingway, as the name suggests, is performed as a blessing for an individual, for example a pregnant mother or a young man going off to war. It is said to be the first chant taught to the 'Earth Surface People' after the emergence into this world.

The creation myth tells us that one of the first things the people do on emerging into this world is to build a hogan – the traditional Navajo home. A major feature of the Blessingway ceremony is the reaffirmation of the *hogan* as an embodiment of the universe and of the Navajo homeland, which is bounded by the four sacred peaks that symbolically hold up the sky. These in turn are associated with the Four Holy Ones, the Four Worlds, and the Four Directions (see Chapter 1). The full creation myth gives Talking God's instructions for building the hogan out of logs, bark and earth. Its packed earth floor represents Mother Earth, its dome-shaped roof Father Sky.

The deities

The Four Holy Ones have their special colours, which stand for the Four Directions: Black Body – east; Blue Body – south; Yellow Body – west; and White Body – north. (Elsewhere the colour of the east is said to be red.) The colour system is almost the same as that used by the Apache. Each god has been ruler of one of the previous worlds, suggesting a model of human evolution whereby each stage is focused on a different spiritual level. The Mirage People are separate from, yet related to, the Four Holy Ones. There are eight of them, suggesting the beginnings of a pantheon in which each of the original four powers is split into two aspects. That they are prepared to marry humans shows that they are of a lower order than the original Holy Ones.

As for Coyote, he seems to be something of an interloper in this story. He is a representative of the trickster archetype (see Chapter 1). As in Norse myth, where the trickster is Loki, even the Holy Ones can have their best-laid plans thrown awry by the element of creative chaos that he introduces into the equation.

The gods' attempt to teach the people through sign language may refer to human efforts to master the art of divination – communication with the divine. The people's failure to read the signs suggests that they are out of touch with the spirit world, which is why it falls to Black Body, God of Fire (related to intuition) to spell the message out to them. The gods' disapproval of the people's lack of cleanliness is a measure of the extent to which they have 'fallen' from the perfection of original creation.

The Holy Wind

The climax of the story is the magical ceremony by which First Man and First Woman are created. The buckskins represent the earth and sky. This echoes myths such as the Maori creation story, in which Papa (earth) and Rangi (sky) produce offspring that are then sandwiched between them. In the Navajo myth, however, the separation between the primal parents – as represented by the buckskins – is effected by the winds.

The Navajo have a concept of *nilchi* or Holy Wind. This refers to the air, the atmosphere, the life-breath and to something more indefinable, which is related to the Christian Holy Spirit. *Nilchi* suffuses the natural world. It gives life, thought, speech and the power of motion and is the universal means of communication. The Navajo believe that it enters the unborn child at conception; when the child takes its first breath, it takes in the surrounding *nilchi*, and thus becomes a complete being. *Nilchi* is said to enter and leave humans through the whorls of the fingertips and toes and through the whorl pattern of the hair on the top of the head. It sits on the tongue, permitting speech. The Navajo also believe that small *nilchi* spirits sit on their ears advising them on correct action – but that these will leave if persistently ignored.

The animating winds blow from the east and the west. East represents birth, or yang; west stands for death, or yin. So life is formed out of this dynamic meeting of opposites and both birth and death are a part of the cycle of life.

Brand new beings

First Man and First Woman are miraculously produced and, like Adam and Eve, in the image of their creators. It is fitting that they are made from corn, because this was the Navajo's staple crop. This is therefore just one step removed from myths in which humans are made from earth, such as the Egyptian myth of Ptah the divine potter. First Woman springs from the yellow (west and yin) ear and First Man from the white (east and yang). Note, however, that eagle feathers, representing spirit, are also involved: man is a spiritual as well as a physical being.

The primal couple's first pair of children are hermaphrodite, like many early beings and deities, suggesting a time of union and self-sufficiency before the division into genders with its attendant sexual desire. The shameful discovery by the other pairs that the gods disapprove of marriage between siblings seems to point to the development of an incest taboo, which is very strong in many tribes.

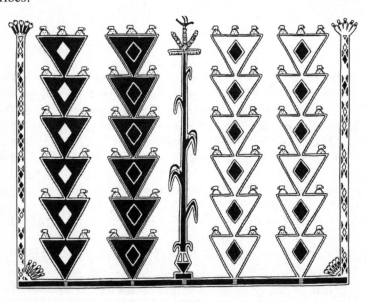

Navajo sand painting. The central corn stalk's three roots grow from an earth symbol. The four columns (two dark, two light) are clouds containing diamond-shaped hailstones. Cloud spirits peep over the clouds. At the bottom is water with seeds; at the sides are rainbow ropes.

5 | CHANGING WOMAN

Changing Woman (Estsanatlehi) is the most respected Navajo deity and is also revered by other south-western tribes. The Chiricahua Apache call her Painted Woman. There are many different accounts of her birth and her marriage to the Sun. This one draws on Leland C. Wyman's *Blessingway*, among other sources.

After the Holy Ones had created First Man and First Woman and the couple had begun to populate the land, everything went well at first. The corn ripened in the sun, the people had plenty to eat and so they sang songs in praise and thanks to the gods. However, when the people had emerged from the three consecutive worlds which had been their previous homes, each time they had brought with them a seed of evil from the world below. So it was that the women of the tribe started abusing themselves with different kinds of animal horns. After a while they realized they had become pregnant, and in their shame they went away so that the men would know nothing about it. Out in the desert among the cactus trees, they gave birth to babies and left them there to die of thirst and be eaten by vultures and coyotes. But the babies did not die; they became monsters.

These monsters grew up and began to breed, and for their food they picked off the people from the outskirts of the village. They became bolder and entered the village, and their greedy appetite increased. It became difficult for the people to go out and tend their corn, and life became very hard.

One day First Man and First Woman heard a voice from the gods telling them what to do. Before dawn they left the village and went to the mountain called Gobernador Knob. Then, as the first rays of the sun broke out of the pink haze of dawn and lit the mountain, First Man held up his medicine bundle in supplication and sang a sacred song. As his voice rose into the sky, a dark cloud gathered out of nowhere and hung over the mountain. The couple quickly prayed, asking Talking God to investigate. He came and climbed the stony peak. At the summit, beneath the cloud, where a rainbow touched the earth, he found a baby girl. She lay on a bed of flowers beneath a softly falling rain.

Talking God carried the child down and gave her to First Man and First Woman. 'Take care of her,' he said. 'She was born of darkness and dawn is her father. Now you will be her parents in their place.'

First Man and First Woman took the child back and showed her to the people. 'She is a sacred child who has entered our time. She is the child of the seasons. We will call her Changing Woman.'

Changing Woman grew up fast. In four days' time she had reached womanhood with her first menstruation, and the people held the first ever puberty ceremony. It was a great occasion. The Holy People came and Talking God conducted the rites. In preparation, Changing Woman was beautifully clothed in a buckskin dress decorated with precious stones from each of the four sacred mountains: white shell, turquoise, abalone and jet. She was blessed with pollen from the dawn and from the evening light, and her hair was bathed in dew. Talking God instructed her to run towards the dawn as far as she could and then to return. As she ran, the dewdrops sprang sparkling from her hair and her jewel dress jingled.

This was repeated on four mornings. When she was not involved in the ceremony, she occupied her time with planning the earth's future and making useful things for the people. In this way she made millstones, brooms, pots and stirring sticks.

At Changing Woman's next menstruation, another ceremony was held, similar to the first. At this ceremony the order of the songs in the Blessingway ceremony was determined. Now Changing Woman was ready to walk the path of life prepared for her.

One day at noon, while she was out alone gathering herbs, a dazzling light appeared and she was forced to look away. With her eyes shielded she was able to make out a handsome man whose body was made of light. He came close and spoke to her: 'Prepare yourself for a great event. In time I will visit you again.'

She ran home and told First Man and First Woman, who seemed to have been expecting this. Next day she met the bright man again. After this she was told to sleep outside the family hogan, with her head to the east and her feet to the west. When she went to sleep the man came to her in her dreams. He lay beside her and she asked who he was.

Softly he replied: 'Don't you know me? You see me every day all around you. I am the inner form of the sun. You were born in my presence.'

The next day she decided to go to a pool where a mountain stream sprayed over a jutting rock. She wanted to bathe because the man might visit her again. She swam, enjoying the cool touch of the water on her skin and then as she lay on a flat rock drying and warming herself, the dazzling brightness appeared and the young man entered between her legs as a warm and penetrating ray of sunlight.

In just nine days, Changing Woman gave birth to twins. The signs in the sky showed that they would be great and sure enough they grew up in twelve days and became the heroes Monster-Slayer and Born-for-Water, who were to save their people from the monsters.

Having brought these two heroes into the world, Changing Woman asked First Man for the medicine bundle that he had raised in supplication to the gods before her birth on the mountain. Then she moved to a hogan built specially for her at the bottom of Huerfano Mountain. Here she conducted the first wedding ceremony: the mating of corn. Eventually she moved to a turquoise palace which the Sun had told her sons to build for her on an island across the ocean to the west. Here in the evening the Sun would visit her after his journey across the land. But by day she often felt lonely, and so she created the Navajo people from her own skin. The four pairs of people she made became the ancestors of the whole tribe.

COMMENTARY

Changing Woman is a personification of the earth, the seasons and even the natural order of the universe. As such, she plays a vital part in the Blessingway ceremony and is the only deity depicted in its sand paintings. Despite embodying the seasons, she has no harsh, wintry 'crone' aspect to her character and appears to be consistently benign in her attitude towards humanity. Since most beings in Navajo myth are paired, a dominant partner being balanced by a subordinate, Changing Woman is in a sense the subordinate of the Sun. Yet it is probably true to say that her power is more gentle, rather than inferior to his. In fact Changing Woman has a subordinate sister, White Shell Woman, just as the Sun has a weaker brother, the Moon.

Monsters of the mind

Changing Woman comes into the world because of the existence of the monsters. It is her destiny to give birth to the twin heroes who will save humanity. These monsters represent the unassimilated, threatening elements of the unconscious. They are especially connected with its desires, as shown by the unnatural self-stimulation of the women. Their use of animal horns runs counter to the correct path of human evolution, not only because it is bestial, but because the horns are dead things that cannot offer a living relationship. Their shame at giving birth to the monsters is linked to repression, which, as Freud noted, tend to make whatever is repressed grow to fearsome proportions and sap the energy available to the psyche. When the monsters start to raid the villages, they are invading the conscious mind.

The symbolism of the birth

The dark cloud under which Changing Woman is born is not ominous. Rather, it symbolizes the integration of the unconscious (water) with spirit (its lofty height). In some Native American myths, a mountain lake carries the same symbolism. The cloud is dark because it is full of water and perhaps because of an association with night. The rainbow under which she is found is, as in the biblical story, a symbol of hope. It represents unity, in that it spans the earth and includes the colours of all four directions. It is also the product of the two forces that the Navajo consider to be essential to conception: light (including warmth) and water (rain, mist and semen). The gentle rain is a blessing, especially in an area with low rainfall for much of the year. As Talking God says, Changing Woman is the child of darkness and dawn. Thus she represents the fruitful union of complementary opposites.

Changing Woman comes to maturity

As is usually the case with divine beings, Changing Woman matures quickly and since most things in Navajo myth are done in fours, it takes her four days. Her puberty ceremony is an initiation, as shown by her running toward the dawn, the place of initiation. Her dress is decorated with the stones of the four sacred mountains, again showing that in her person she draws together the whole universe. She is blessed with pollen, which as the agent of fertilization is regarded as very holy by the Navajo.

Navajo girls traditionally marry young and so it is not long after reaching puberty that Changing Woman has her first encounter with the Sun. He is her ideal counterpart, the divine hero, the positive animus within the female psyche; hence his appearance to her in dreams. He also represents spirit come to impregnate the physical world. In this context, note that to the Navajo each thing in the world has its 'inner form' and so the Sun is able to leave his physical form lighting up the world, while his inner form, his spiritual essence, visits Changing Woman.

There are several different versions of Changing Woman's impregnation by the Sun. In the Apache version she is inspired to climb a hill and build a *wickiup* (shelter) with four poles, where the first rays of the sun will strike in the morning. She sleeps there and as the sun rises it shines between her legs and causes her first menstrual period, after which she becomes pregnant. She conceives a son and calls him Monster-Slayer. It is four days later that she is impregnated again, this time by Water-Old-Man, and conceives the other son, Born of Water. This Apache version makes more explicit the distinction between the two elements involved in the conception: sunlight (spirit) and water (the unconscious). In the Navajo version given here, the two are combined.

Changing Woman has already fulfilled a role as culture heroine, providing the Navajo with useful inventions, and now she has given birth to two sons destined to save the people. While she is still important, her major roles have now been fulfilled. It is probably for this reason that she is persuaded (in some versions with difficulty) to move to a house in the west. The west in many myths worldwide is the place where gods are 'pensioned off', as in the case of Cronus in Greek myth after he is deposed by Zeus. However, there is no clear evidence of the Navajo moving from a matriarchal to a patriarchal society and in fact Navajo family organization is still matrilineal. Moreover, Changing Woman continues to play a vital part in ritual. Therefore it seems that her removal to the west signifies an honourable and active retirement rather than a deposition.

6 | THE MONSTER BOYS AND THE FLOOD

This myth of the Caddo tribe features problem children and a world deluge.

There was once a woman who was about to give birth. As she was the wife of a chief, there was particular interest in the coming event, especially as she had grown so large: 'Perhaps we're going to be blessed with twins,' said her husband hopefully.

The woman's time came and she went alone to a creek and built a small hut of grasses, equipped with a clinging pole to assist her in her labour. But the woman did not have twins; instead, after a difficult labour, she gave birth to four little monsters, each with four legs and arms. She washed in the creek and returned to her village. When the elders saw the babies, they frowned and shook their heads: 'These misshapen children will bring bad luck. Surely it would be better to kill them now, for the sake of the village. If we let them grow up, who knows what they will become?'

'No one is going to take my children away,' the mother said firmly. 'They'll grow into fine young men – you'll see.'

The monsters grew much faster than other children and began to cause injuries and create havoc everywhere they went, upturning tipis and ripping up buffalo robes. A wise elder who could see into the misty future spoke to the mother: 'I know this is hard for you, but you must kill these monster children before it's too late.'

'They're just behaving as all children do', she said, dismissively.

In time the monsters grew huge and began to kill and eat villagers. When this happened, the men of the village took up their weapons and rushed at the monsters to kill them. But the wise man's prediction had come true: the monsters were now too powerful to be killed and the men had to retreat in shame.

The monsters kept growing and terrorizing the villagers. Then one day they went into the centre of the circle of huts forming the village and stood back to back facing towards the four directions. In this position they grew together and became one. But they could still reach out and grab people with their enormous arms that stretched far beyond the village into the surrounding countryside. However, being joined, they could not bend down; so the villagers sheltered at their feet, out of their reach. Meanwhile the monsters grew up so that their heads touched the sky.

Now the wise man who had earlier predicted that the monsters would get out of hand heard a mysterious voice telling him to plant a hollow reed in the ground. He did this and the reed grew very quickly into a thick cane. Now the voice spoke again: 'I will flood the earth. When you and your wife see all the birds of the world form a great cloud flying from north to south, this will be the sign. Then you must both climb inside the hollow cane, naked as when you came into the earth. Take with you a pair of every kind of good animal.'

Before long, the sky began to grow dark in the day and the man looked up and saw a great cloud of birds blotting out the sun and flying south. He and his wife lost no time in gathering up the pairs of animals and climbing into the cane. Even as they did, the skies opened and a downpour commenced that in a few days flooded the earth, leaving only the tip of the hollow cane and the heads of the four monsters sticking out.

From inside the cane, the man heard the voice again: 'Now I will send Turtle to destroy those monsters!'

The monsters, in the meantime, were getting worried. They shouted to each other above the sound of the rain: 'I'm getting so tired with all this swirling water. I can't stand up for much longer.'

Now Turtle dived down and began to dig around and underneath the monsters' feet, so that soon, with the strong currents pushing too, the monsters sank beneath the waves and drowned. They fell to the north, south, east and west, creating the four directions.

Gradually the waters went down, revealing the mountain peaks and then the rest of the land. The wind and sun dried out the earth and soon the man and his wife were able to lead the animals out. The man and his wife slept and when they awoke, herbs and plants had sprung up. The next morning they woke to find trees and bushes. Now they had wood for bows and arrow and for the fire. After the third night grass carpeted the earth and animals grazed on it.

After the fourth night the couple woke to find themselves inside a grass hut. They stepped outside into the sunshine and found a cob of corn. The voice now spoke to them again, saying: 'This will be your holy food.' It told the woman how to plant, tend and harvest the corn. 'Now you have everything you need,' it continued. 'You will have children and they too will have children. If ever you plant corn and something else grows, then you will know that the world is about to end.'

And this was the last they ever heard of the voice.

COMMENTARY

This myth combines the themes of monster children, deluge and emergence into the present world. It is common in Native American myths for the last two to be linked, as in the Jicarilla Apache creation myth discussed earlier.

The monster children are similar to the monsters born to the women in the Navajo creation myth (see Chapter 5), but in the Caddo myth there is no suggestion that the mother is to blame. In fact in standing up for her children she is being a good mother. The monsters symbolize unassimilated, socially and personally destructive tendencies in the unconscious. The recommendation by the elders that the boys be killed for the good of the tribe represents repression. Infanticide was in fact carried out by the Caddo when children were unwanted. In psychic terms the reason for their not being killed at this point is that the unconscious impulses which they represent already have an overwhelming vitality. It is interesting that the father plays so little part in the story. This is reminiscent of the Navajo story, in which the monsters have no fathers at all. The over-dominance of the mother could hint at cosmic or psychic imbalance being the root cause of the problem.

The fusion of the four monster boys suggests a counter-evolutionary development, particularly given that when they are forced apart they become the Four Directions, whose existence is so much a part of Native American cosmology. In fusing they become like other many-headed monsters, such as the Greek Hydra.

The Caddo believed in an omnipotent deity, Ayanat Caddi, or Great Captain, and the voice that speaks to the wise man is his. One cannot avoid comparison with the biblical tale of Noah, in which another omnipotent God gives instructions which are remarkably similar, particularly in relation to the saving of one pair of each animal species. Both myths could be interpreted in terms of the evolution of consciousness from the sea of the unconscious, although they could also be based on a prehistoric flood.

The birds that the Caddo deity sends as a sign refer to divination, which is a means of accessing the intuition through the interpretation of natural events. Birds are a popular method because their ability to fly links them imaginatively with the spirit and because of their varied behaviour (such as flying in different directions), which lends itself to interpretation.

The turtle is found in many Native American myths, usually as a world saviour. An Ojibway myth tells how Turtle rescued the earth from a flood by diving down and coming up with enough earth on his back for people to live on. This contains the familiar theme of self-sacrifice, since Turtle drowns. Many Native Americans now refer to the world as 'Turtle Island'. In the Caddo myth, as far as we know, Turtle survives. The turtle is thought of as a magical animal because of its ability to live in two worlds – on land and in water. It is also associated with the Four Directions because its legs appear to point towards them.

The last part of the myth is typical of 'culture' myths in which deities teach humans how to live. The prophecy relating to the end of the world is somewhat enigmatic, although with current developments in genetic engineering, it could be about to come true. Taken less literally, it could simply be a way of stating an essential law of nature that the fruit grows according to its seed.

7 | **ARROW BOY**

This myth is important to the Cheyenne, as it tells the story of how they received their sacred medicine bundle and many of their rituals and sacred songs. It is comparable to the Lakota myth of White Buffalo Woman, in which the sacred object is the pipe.

A young man and woman were married and the woman became pregnant. After the usual period of time had elapsed without the woman giving birth, the people began to wonder. After a year they were baffled. When, after another three years, she gave birth to a handsome boy, they expected him to have special powers.

Soon after this the boy's parents died and he was adopted by his grandmother. He grew up fast and could walk and talk after a few months. When the people gave him a soft buffalo robe, he thanked them and then turned it inside out so that the hair was on the outside, in the style of a medicine man and this was how he wore it when, at the age of ten, he was permitted to take part in a magical dance.

He entered the great buffalo hide lodge of the medicine men, glancing at the magical figures painted around its entrance flap. Inside was a tightly packed group of men, seated on the ground. The head medicine man nodded to the boy and asked where he wanted to sit. Without asking, the boy sat down beside this man. At the same time he instructed the man who had shown him in: 'Paint my body red with ochre, and draw black circles round my face, wrists and ankles.'

The men now took it in turns to demonstrate their power. When it was the boy's turn, he took some sweetgrass and burned it. The fragrant smoke drifted around the lodge. Then the boy took his sinew bowstring and passed it through the smoke in each of the four directions – east, south, west and north. He asked two men to help him: they were to tie the bowstring around his neck, cover him up with his robe and pull as hard as they could on the bowstring. They did this, and on their second attempt the bowstring cut through the boy's neck. His head rolled out from under the robe, and the men put it back.

Now the men lifted the robe to find, in place of a boy, a wrinkled old man. They covered him with the robe and this time on removing the robe they discovered a skeleton. They cast the robe over the skeleton and took it away. This time there was nothing. The fourth time they cast and removed the robe and there sat the boy, smiling quietly as if nothing had happened. The men were used to seeing wonders, but they all agreed that this boy had exceptional powers.

After this the tribe moved camp to hunt the buffalo. After a big kill, the boy said to some other boys: 'Come, let's go and look for calves returning to the place where they last saw their mothers.'

The boys went with their bows and found several calves, killing one with their flint-tipped arrows. 'I want to keep the skin for a robe,' said the boy and so they skinned it carefully, keeping the head and hooves intact.

When they had almost finished, they saw a tall man approaching with a team of dogs pulling a sled. It was Young Wolf, the head chief. 'Congratulations, boys,' he said. 'Now run along and leave this buffalo to me.'

The other boys did as they were told, but the wonderful boy told Young Wolf, 'I just want the hide,' and kept on working. The chief pushed him away but the boy quietly returned to his work. Then Young Wolf flung the boy to one side and the boy picked himself up and continued skinning – but this time he cut off a leg at the knee, leaving the hoof attached. When the angry chief pushed the boy away a third time, the boy whirled his buffalo hoof and brought it down on Young Wolf's head, killing him.

When the people of the camp heard of this, the men met and decided that they must kill the boy who had killed their chief. They went to the lodge of the boy's grandmother, where she was cooking buffalo meat in a pot, which sat on a glowing fire. As the boy sat waiting for his meal, suddenly the whole tipi was flung up and the men rushed to seize him. Quickly he kicked over the steaming pot, so that its contents emptied onto the fire. The boy was enveloped in the cloud of white smoke and rose with it through the tipi's smoke hole.

Going outside and looking around, the men saw the boy off in the distance. They pursued him, but even their fastest runners could never get any closer to him. Four times they tried and then they gave up.

'Leave him,' they said to each other. 'He has great powers and we shouldn't provoke him.'

Still, they watched for the boy and one day they saw him on a hilltop. The whole camp came to see him. He appeared five times, each time dressed differently. First he came as a Red Shield warrior in a buffalo head-dress, then as a Coyote warrior painted black and yellow and with eagle feathers on his head, then as a Dog Men warrior in a feather head-dress and carrying an eagle-bone whistle, a rattle, and a bow and arrows. The fourth time he came as a Hoof Rattle warrior, painted and carrying a rattle and a long spear. Finally he came painted white, with a white owl skin on his forehead.

After this great show, the boy disappeared. People gradually forgot him and at the same time the buffalo disappeared and the people starved. But the boy was not dead as some thought; he had gone into the western mountains and travelled alone among the peaks. As he approached a wooded slope, a stone rolled aside to reveal an entrance and he passed through it into the earth, the stone rolled back behind him.

The boy once again found himself in a group of medicine men. But this time he was in a chamber dimly lit by magical fire. The walls glistened and all around him the eyes of the men watched him closely. There was one empty seat in the circle and the leader of the men gestured towards it. Hanging over it was a bundle of arrows wrapped in fox skin. 'If you accept this seat,' said the man seriously, 'you must take the bundle back to your tribe. But first you will stay here and be instructed in our mysteries, so that you can become your tribe's great prophet.'

The boy accepted the bundle and the responsibility that went with it and the men were happy. They took down the bundle and showed him its sacred songs and ceremonies and its four arrows of power. Here, too, he received his new name, Arrow Boy.

Arrow Boy spent four years in the mountain, learning magic and prophecy. All this time his people were starving, reduced to eating herbs and mushrooms. One day, when the people were close to despair, five children were out gathering what little food they could find. Arrow Boy suddenly appeared in their midst. 'Put away those herbs and mushrooms,' he cried. 'I caused the famine because I was angry with the people, but now I will give you meat. Bring me some buffalo bones.'

The children, though weak, did as Arrow Boy said. He raised his hands over the sun-bleached bones and as he sang a magical song, the bones grew a covering of fresh meat. He gave the best parts to the children and then sent them to tell their people that Arrow Boy had returned.

When the children arrived in the camp still licking buffalo grease from their lips and told their parents what had happened, there was a stir of excitement. Then the people discovered Arrow Boy already in a lodge, lying down and painted red all over. They saw his bundle and knew that the young man had power. He sat up and told them to camp in a circle, erecting a large tipi in the centre. He called the medicine men together and here he taught them all the sacred songs that he had learned. When he came to the song about the fourth arrow, it was dark. As he finished the song the ground began to vibrate and then a great thundering grew all around. The buffalo had returned.

The next morning the plains were covered with buffalo and the people were able to kill all they wanted. From this time, thanks to the sacred arrow bundle, the Cheyenne had plenty to eat and became a powerful nation.

COMMENTARY

The hero of this myth, like many heroes worldwide, has a mysterious birth and a prodigious childhood. He is also typical of one type of hero in that he is quickly orphaned and therefore has to carve out his own destiny without help from his parents. This also emphasizes that he is really a child of spirit. He shows his spiritual calling early on, wearing his robe in the manner of the medicine men and having the knowledge and innate authority to instruct the man at the lodge entrance as to how he should be painted in preparation for his first display of power. The colours may relate to the directions of north (red) and west (black). North among many Plains tribes is the direction of spiritual growth and of the Buffalo Nation. West is the direction of the Thunder Beings, who are associated with battle. These colours therefore reveal that he is holy and is about to do battle.

The first part of the demonstration resembles the Yuwipi ceremony of the Lakota, a tribe closely allied to the Cheyenne, whom they call 'the Brother People'. This is a healing ceremony in which the medicine man is tightly tied up in a blanket with rawhide thongs. The healing spirits are encouraged by darkness and with chanting and rattles. According to a 1918 account by anthropologist Frances Densmore, the man is eventually found untied but wedged between the poles at the top of the tipi. Significantly she describes this ceremony as one in which the healer proves his supernatural powers to the sick patient; in the myth, the boy is proving his powers to the medicine men.

The boy's ability to lose his head and then regain it may represent the shamanistic power to lose control of one's ego, for the purposes of opening up to the spirits and then regain it. The rest of the display seems to demonstrate the boy's power over old age, death and even non-existence. The boy demonstrates self-control, audacity and physical prowess in killing the chief who decides to commandeer his buffalo. Then he demonstrates his spiritual power by rising through the smoke hole in his grandmother's tipi. The smoke hole is where the poles of the tipi cross over. This creates two vortices or cone shapes. According to some Native American commentators these represent an exchange between the spiritual and material worlds. Human beings are at the apex between these two worlds. When the boy passes through the smoke hole he is going to the spirit world. This is emphasized by the inability of the runners to draw any closer to him: he is on another plane.

(Something similar happens in a story of the Buddha and in Celtic mythical encounters with Otherwordly beings.)

The boy disappears for a while, presumably communing with the spirits, and is then seen as several different types of warrior. Many tribes had warrior societies with their own songs and customs and often their own roles both in battle and in daily life. One of the Cheyenne warrior societies in whose guise the boy appears, the Dog Men (or Dog Soldiers), was responsible for policing and especially for preventing young men from endangering the tribe by prematurely attacking an enemy in order to gain personal glory. The Dog Men took their name from the practice in which several would be chosen to carry a rawhide leash and wooden stake into battle. If necessary they would stake themselves to the ground by their leash and fight a rearguard action while the rest of the band retreated or until they were replaced. The appearance of the boy five times may relate to the Four Directions, plus the Centre.

The mountains which the boy visits may be the Black Hills, sacred to both the Cheyenne and the Lakota. At any rate they represent a spiritual ascent. The cave combines this with a symbolic *descent* into the realm of the unconscious, which is also the womb of Mother Earth. In a sense the boy is reborn here, which is why he now takes a new name, Arrow Boy. The sacred arrow bundle is both a token of his own initiation and a fetish object which the tribe invests with spiritual power. The four arrows probably refer to the Four Directions. This bundle is said to exist still, in the safekeeping of Cheyenne elders.

When Arrow Boy brings back the bundle and teaches his tribe the all-important songs and rituals, the Cheyenne's relationship with the spirit world is renewed and the immediate proof of this is that the buffalo return.

8 | WHITE BUFFALO WOMAN

This is a central myth of the Plains tribes, especially the Lakota, or Sioux. It tells how the Lakota first received their sacred pipe and the ceremony in which to use it. It has often been related, for example by Black Elk, Lame Deer and Looks for Buffalo.

In the days before the Lakota had horses on which to hunt the buffalo, food was often scarce. One summer when the Lakota nation had camped together, there was very little to eat. Two young men of the Itazipcho band – the 'Without-Bows' – decided they would rise early and look for game. They left the camp while the dogs were still yawning and set out across the plain, accompanied only by the song of the yellow meadowlark.

After a while the day began to grow warm. Crickets chirruped in the waving grass, prairie dogs darted into their holes as the braves approached, but still there was no real game. So the young men made towards a little hill from which they would see further across the vast expanse of level prairie. Reaching it, they shielded their eyes and scanned the distance, but what they saw coming out of the growing heat haze was something bright, that seemed to go on two legs, not four. In a while they could see that it was a very beautiful woman in shining white buckskin.

As the woman came closer, they could see that her buckskin was wonderfully decorated with sacred designs in rainbow-coloured porcupine quills. She carried a bundle on her back and a fan of fragrant sage leaves in her hand. Her jet-black hair was loose, except for a single strand tied with buffalo fur. Her eyes were full of light and power and the young men were transfixed.

Now one of the men was filled with a burning desire. 'What a woman!' he said sideways to his friend. 'And all alone on the prairie. I'm going to make the most of this!'

'You fool,' said the other. 'This woman is holy.'

But the foolish one had made up his mind and when the woman beckoned him towards her, he needed no second invitation. As he reached out for her, they were both enveloped in a great cloud. When it lifted, the woman stood there, while at her feet was nothing but a pile of bones with terrible snakes writhing among them.

'Behold,' said the woman to the good brave. 'I am coming to your people with a message from Tatanka Oyate, the Buffalo Nation. Return to Chief Standing Hollow Horn and tell him what you have seen. Tell him to prepare a tipi large enough for all his people and to get ready for my coming.'

The young man ran back across the prairie and was gasping for breath as he reached his camp. With a small crowd of people already following him, he found Standing Hollow Horn and told him what had happened and that the woman was coming. The chief ordered several tipis to be combined into one big enough for his band. The people waited excitedly for the woman to arrive.

After four days the scouts posted to watch for the holy woman saw something coming towards them in a beautiful manner from across the prairie. Then suddenly the woman was in the great lodge, walking round it in a sunwise direction. She stopped before Standing Hollow Horn in the west of the lodge and held her bundle before him in both hands.

'Look on this,' she said, 'and always love and respect it. No one who is impure should ever touch this bundle, for it contains the sacred pipe.'

She unrolled the skin bundle and took out a pipe and a small round stone which she put down on the ground, saying:

With this pipe you will walk on the earth, which is your grandmother and your mother. The earth is sacred and so is every step that you take on her. The bowl of the pipe is of red stone; it is the earth. Carved into it and facing the centre is the buffalo calf, who stands for all the four-leggeds. The stem is of wood, which stands for all that grows on the earth. These twelve hanging feathers from the Spotted Eagle stand for all the winged creatures. All these living things of the universe are the children of Mother Earth. You are all joined as one family and you will be reminded of this when you smoke the pipe. Treat this pipe and the earth with respect and your people will increase and prosper.'

The woman told them that seven circles carved on the stone represented the seven rites in which the people would learn to use the sacred pipe. The first was for the rite of 'keeping the soul', which she now taught them. The remaining rites they would learn in due course.

The woman made as if to leave the lodge, but then she turned and spoke to Standing Hollow Horn again. 'This pipe will carry you to the end. Remember that in me there are four ages. I am going now, but I will look on your people in every age and at the end I will return.'

She now walked slowly around the lodge in a sunwise direction. The people were silent and filled with awe. Even the hungry young children watched her, their eyes alive with wonder. Then she left. But after she had walked a short distance, she faced the people again and sat down on the prairie. The people gazing after her were amazed to see that when she stood up she had become a young red and brown buffalo calf. The calf walked further into the prairie and then lay down and rolled over, looking back at the people. When she stood up she was a white buffalo. The white buffalo walked on until she was a bright speck in the distant prairie and then rolled over again and became a black buffalo. This buffalo walked away, stopped, bowed to the four directions of the earth and finally disappeared over the hill.

COMMENTARY

To the Lakota this is probably the most important of all their myths. It has also become a spiritual focus for Plains tribes generally. It has three main aspects: White Buffalo Woman herself and what she represents, both historically and in the present day; the encounter with the two young men; and the importance of the sacred pipe and the ritual that goes with it.

The spirit woman

This is the only myth in which White Buffalo Woman appears. Moreover, there is no attempt to create a whole life story for her and she has no identifiable family or husband, unlike the Navajo's Changing Woman. She is altogether mysterious, appearing on the distant horizon, bringing her gifts, and then departing. In her self-sufficiency and virgin inviolability she is like the Greek goddesses Athene and Artemis, although since the coming of the Native American Church, many Native people have identified her with the Virgin Mary.

Certainly she is a powerful anima figure, a maiden goddess who springs direct, untarnished, from the spirit world. She is also a culture goddess in that she brings the all-important fetish object, the sacred pipe, as well as teaching the people how to use it to remain in communication with the spirit world. She is said to come from the north, which is the home of the Buffalo Nation (Tatanka Oyate) and the place of health and spiritual growth through self-discipline and endurance.

She is of course closely identified with the buffalo. For the Lakota, as for most Plains tribes, the buffalo was a vital source of food and clothing, as well as providing most of the material goods of everyday life. Tools were made from its bones, rattles from its hooves, tipis from its hide. The Plains tribes also had a close spiritual relationship with the buffalo, as inferred by the Lakota emergence myth in which the medicine man turns himself into a buffalo to feed the tribe (see page 00).

The Ghost Dance religion, which tragically led to the Wounded Knee Massacre, had as one of its aims the restoration of the buffalo. It met with failure, but there is a prophecy, believed by many modern Lakota, that when four white buffalo have been born, then the old ways will return and the earth will be saved. White Buffalo Woman herself, in the myth, promises to return 'at the end'.

The encounter

The two young men show two very different attitudes towards the spirit world. One is oblivious to the woman's power and is reduced to bones by this encounter with spirit power for which he is totally unprepared. Joseph Epes Brown, in *The Sacred Pipe*, quotes the famous Lakota medicine man Black Elk's explanation of the foolish man's fate: 'Any man who is attached to the senses and to the things of this world, is one who lives in ignorance and is being consumed by the snakes which represent his own passions.'

This makes the important point that the foolish man's action stands for more than just sexual desire.

The pipe

The pipe is extremely important in Lakota ritual. It is the symbolic means of making an exchange between humanity and the spirit world. Hence when smoked it is always offered to the Four Directions. The smoke is regarded as rising up to the spirit world.

The Plains tribes still make their pipe bowls from red pipestone found only in a quarry in south-west Minnesota. The dark red stone is said to be the congealed blood of those killed in the flood and it is also a reminder of the blood sacrificed by the creator Inyan in order to make the world. In addition it is the colour of the earth in much of Lakota territory. Lastly, it is the colour of the 'red road' associated with the north, the direction from which White Buffalo Woman comes. This refers to what in Christian terms is the 'path of righteousness'.

When the White Buffalo Woman enters the lodge she walks around it in the solar directions, to meet the chief in the west (opposite the east, place of dawn and therefore of enlightenment). The spotted eagle feathers on the pipe are symbols of transcendent solar spiritual power. His feathers are equated with rays of the sun. As Joseph Epes Brown says, when a Lakota wears the eagle-feathered war bonnet, he 'actually becomes the eagle, which is to say that he identifies himself, his real Self, with Wakan Tanka'. Thus when the Ghost Dancers sang, 'The Spotted Eagle is coming to carry me away,' they were referring to spiritual transcendence of the material world.

9 STONE BOY

This Lakota myth, among other things, explains the invention of the sweatlodge. The version below is based on several variations, including early twentieth-century accounts by George Sword and Henry Crow Dog. Charlotte Black Elk, a Lakota oral historian, used her version of the story in a statement given at the Sioux Nation Black Hills Act hearings in the US Senate (1986), stating that her aim was to show that the model of: 'traditional Ikce (Lakota) philosophical principles and theological concepts for organizational design and management practice is one the Lakota have used for thousands of generations and is still appropriate, particularly for the Black Hills.'

Many years ago, there was a girl who lived with her four brothers. They moved around to wherever game was plentiful and in this way they came to set up camp in the bottom of a canyon. Here it was cool in the summer and sheltered from the cold winds of winter. There was also fresh water in a stream, where deer would come to drink in the evening. Each day the men went out hunting and the girl stayed and did jobs around the camp. She looked forward to their return, especially as it often seemed to her that, despite its advantages, there was something unsettling about this place. She would hear voices rustling in the leaves and footsteps outside the tipi when there was no one there.

Then one day the eldest brother failed to return from hunting.

'We lost sight of him in the trees for a moment, and then he was gone,' said one of the other three.

The next day the remaining three brothers went out hunting, hoping to see their lost brother. But this time another brother mysteriously disappeared. Next day two brothers went out and only one returned in the evening. The girl was unhappy and worried. She and her surviving brother, the youngest, sat together round the fire wondering what to do, and what could have happened to the other brothers.

'If you go out hunting on your own, I'm afraid you'll disappear like the others,' said the girl sadly.

'But if I stay here, we'll both starve,' answered the brother.

So the next day the fourth brother took his bow and arrows and waved goodbye to his anxious sister as she stood in the entrance of the tipi. Soon he was out of sight.

That day the girl kept herself busy, fetching water, skinning, and weaving. When the sun was low over the treeline, she began to worry. When the first owls began to call, her heart grew heavy. And when thick night blanketed the canyon and her brother had still not returned, she was afraid and wept, knowing he was lost like the others.

When dawn came, the girl had hardly slept. She left the tipi, climbed out of the canyon and went up a nearby hill, hoping to see a sign of her brothers or even to receive a vision telling her where they were. But there was no sign – not even a whiff of distant smoke, and no vision came. Despite her grief she thought she had better eat something, and in her pocket she thought she felt a bean. It was hard, but she put it in her mouth and swallowed it. And as it went down she realized that in fact it had been a stone.

'Now perhaps I'll die,' she said to herself, afraid, but thinking that she might be better off dead. But instead, she gradually began to feel calm and happy.

After three more days alone, although still strangely calm, she was weak with hunger and passed out as she stood to leave the tipi. When she regained consciousness she was shocked to find blood all around her, as if someone had died. But in fact just the opposite was the case. In a moment she heard the cry of a baby; propping herself up with difficulty, she found him lying near her.

The child seemed strong. He had shining eyes and reminded the girl of her brothers. She found some dried meat and ate that and then was able to dig for roots. So she was able to regain enough strength to feed the baby. She named him Stone Boy, because she realized that he must have been born because she swallowed the stone on the hill.

Stone Boy grew very fast and in no time at all he was making his own bows and hunting rabbits for the cooking pot. One day he came in to find his mother crying and asked her what was the matter.

'You used to have four uncles,' she said. 'But they all disappeared and never came back.' She told him the circumstances of his birth and the boy was thoughtful.

The next day he announced: 'I'm going to find my uncles.'

His mother was worried that she would now lose her son as she had done her brothers, but Stone Boy reassured her. 'I will return, and I'll bring my uncles with me.'

So saying, he took his bow and some dried meat and left the camp. The boy wandered on for three days, until on the evening of the fourth day he saw smoke drifting over the trees. He hurried towards this and came upon a tipi standing on its own. As he approached, he could smell food. Then a beautiful woman – the first he had seen other than his own mother – emerged from the tipi. Her eyes flashed as she saw him and she beckoned him over.

'What are you doing in these parts?' she asked. 'Following a deer, perhaps?'

'No,' answered the boy. 'I'm looking for my four uncles. Have you seen them?'

She seemed to be thinking. 'I'm afraid I haven't,' she answered. 'But come in and eat anyway. You must be hungry.'

This was true, so Stone Boy shared the woman's meal. While he was eating, he noticed four big bundles wrapped in hides and tied tight with thongs. They lay to one side of the tipi.

'What are those?' he asked her.

'Never you mind,', she replied, and dismissing the subject she directed him to a buffalo robe on which he could spend the night if he wished. Then she went outside and the boy seized the opportunity to investigate the bundles. They were heavy and seemed to be shaped like men.

As he was looking the woman came in and as soon as she saw what he was doing, she changed into a fierce-looking, witch-like old woman with wild grey hair. She reached for a skinning knife and rushed towards Stone Boy, but he was too quick for her. He jumped out of her way, picked up a rock from beside the fire, and threw it hard at the woman. It hit her on the head and she fell lifeless to the ground.

Stone Boy took the skinning knife and began to cut open the four big bundles. In each of them he found a man's body, but pale, stiff and dried up. Stone Boy guessed that these were his uncles, but he had no idea how to bring them back to life. Wondering what to do, he wandered outside the tipi and sat down.

As he sat he heard a voice. 'Stone Boy,' it said, 'you are one of us. Listen.'

He looked and saw that the voice was coming from a pile of stones. He went to it and the stones told him to build a round-topped lodge out of willow sticks and cover it with hides and to place the dried-up bodies inside it, with some water. He was then to build a fire and heat the rocks and take them inside the lodge using deer antlers, closing the flap behind him so that it was dark. He did this and poured water on the hot rocks as they instructed him and the lodge filled with steam.

As the lodge heated up, the bodies began to move a little and then to breathe and then to sing. When he opened the flap and let in the light, he could see his uncles properly at last. 'Thank you, nephew,' they said, smiling. 'We are pleased to be alive again!'

So Stone Boy and his uncles returned to the family lodge and all were happy to be reunited. And the people have carried out the sweatlodge ceremony, *inipi*, ever since.

COMMENTARY

This is in part an explanatory myth, in that it recounts the origins of the sweatlodge, but it is also about the importance of family relations and about creation from the first principle of stone, as described in the Lakota creation myth earlier in this book.

The cosmic family unit

The story begins with the vague feeling that 'something is not right', because of the unexplained voices and footsteps and indeed this is the case: the initial cosmic balance is about to be disturbed. Charlotte Black Elk refers to the sister and brothers as a 'family of choice': they have chosen to live as a family, but are not necessarily related biologically. Certainly they are an unusual family, with no parents and no marriages. It also seems strange at first that they do not live as part of a tribal group. However, this is a common situation in Native American myths and it may be that the family's isolation is simply a means of focusing our attention on them alone. Charlotte Black Elk places the story after the Tagluzza Topa (cleansing), a cataclysmic event something like the flood found in other myths. This may also account for their isolation, but it also creates the conditions for upheaval, out of which springs renewal.

This family unit also has cosmic dimensions. It has the same composition as the family in 'The Girl who was the Ring' (Chapter 18) and in both cases the four brothers represent the Four Directions, while the sister stands for the point of synthesis and harmony at their centre. (Note, however, that the Henry Crow Dog version has an extra brother.) The tipi itself, where the girl remains each day, is an extension of this concept. She seems to be passive, simply waiting for her brothers to return, but then when all four have disappeared, she reveals her active aspect by going to look for them. She is also the agent of renewal, in that she gives birth to Stone Boy. In this respect she resembles the Navajo's Changing Woman, who does not kill monsters herself, but gives birth to sons who do.

When the sister is left alone, she has, according to Jacqueline F. Keeler (*Stone Boy: A New Interpretation*), lost her 'locative space'. Without the brothers as Four Directions, she is no longer a centre point. She has become like Han, the dark void at the beginning of the Lakota creation.

Birth from a stone

Henry Crow Dog's version has the girl swallowing a stone in order
to kill herself, which has the virtue of making new life spring out of
despair (especially at a time when many Native Americans were in
deep despair on the reservations). A version recounted by
nineteenth-century ethnologist Marie McLaughlin (who was of
mixed blood, but married into white society) describes the girl
throwing a pebble into water, from which the baby grows. Here the
feminine element of water replaces the womb.

All versions have the essential feature of the boy being born from
stone. This is a further link between this story and the creation
myth, in which Inyan (stone) creates the universe from his lifeblood. In the version of the story given here, the connection with
blood is emphasized by the blood that the sister discovers when she
has given birth.

Stone Boy's quest

Like most other mythical heroes, Stone Boy grows up fast, leaves
his mother and goes off on his chosen quest. Many archetypal
heroes go in search of the father, but Stone Boy has no father in the
conventional sense. Instead he looks for the nearest human thing
that he has to a father – his uncles. In the process he encounters and
defeats the negative anima in the form of the double-faced witch
woman and then finds his metaphorical father in the talking stones.

The woman whom Stone Boy meets is a form of ogress, the
devouring mother. In Henry Crow Dog's version the woman is
clearly a crone: she is old and ugly from the start and offers him a
grubby old buffalo robe to sleep on. She complains that she has a
backache and asks him to massage her back by walking on it. When
he feels something sharp sticking out of her dress, he assumes it is
the weapon used to kill his uncles and therefore kill the hag. In
some versions the negative anima role is taken by an evil sister who
tries to use the uncles' bodies to make something inanimate: a robe
in a version by Ella Deloria, and a shield in one by former medicine
man George Sword. As Jacqueline Keeler says, this is a reversal of

the creation myth in which Maka (Mother Earth) makes a 'robe of creation' from the life-giving powers of family relationships.

In the version given here, the woman's beautiful face conceals an ugly one. This links her to Anog Ite (Two-Faced Woman; see page 10). Stone Boy appropriately kills her with his namesake: a stone.

The sweatlodge

Inipi (the sweatlodge) is said to be the oldest Lakota rite, the one which the Lakota already had before the coming of White Buffalo Woman. Briefly, a small dome-shaped lodge is made out of willow branches, covered with hides (or nowadays blankets and tarpaulins), so that inside it is completely dark. There is a buffalo skull altar outside, and a fire in which the rocks are heated before being brought in. Water is poured on to create steam. Physically this is something like a sauna, but it has a great spiritual significance as a means of purification. The shape of the lodge and the darkness imitate the womb, and the participants are said to be reborn on emerging. (For a fuller account, see my *Timeless Wisdom of the Native Americans*.)

Thus the four brothers are physically brought back to life, but they are also reborn spiritually.

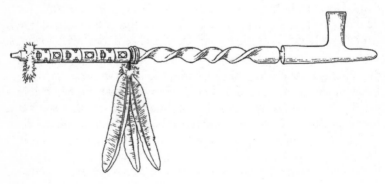

Lakota pipe

10 | RABBIT BOY

This is a myth of the White River Sioux, but other tribes have versions of it, some calling it 'Blood-Clot Boy' or 'Blood-Clot Man'.

In the days when animals could sometimes change themselves into people and people into animals, there lived a good-natured rabbit. One day he was strolling along and came upon a little blood clot, like a blister, lying on the path. Playfully, he started to kick it around like a ball. With all this play, the spirit of motion entered into the ball of blood, and it started to change shape. It grew little arms and hands and a beating heart and before long, the rabbit stopped kicking, because he could see that it had grown into a little boy – Rabbit Boy.

The rabbit took the boy to meet his wife and she was delighted with him. In fact the kind-hearted couple loved the boy as if he was their own, fitting him out with a buckskin shirt decorated with porcupine quills. They boy grew up very happily with his rabbit family, but when he had nearly reached manhood the rabbit, now old, sat the boy down to speak to him: 'My boy, the time has come. You think you're a rabbit like me, but in fact you're something else – a human. You need to be with other humans. Much as we love you, you must find your own people.'

So Rabbit Boy left the rabbits and before long came into a human village. The people stared at this newcomer in his beautiful clothes and asked him where he had come from. 'Another village', he answered, not wishing to reveal more.

Rabbit Boy settled into the village, his kind heart and cheerful manner making him popular with everyone. In time he had a mysterious vision, in which he was pitting himself against the sun and always winning. So when a girl of the village fell in love with him, everyone hoped that a young man with such spirit power would marry into the village.

There was, however, one person with whom Rabbit Boy was not popular. This was Iktome, the Spider Man. Iktome was a wicked cheat and a trickster and he wanted the girl for himself. So he went around blackening the name of Rabbit Boy. 'Look at Rabbit Boy,' he sneered. 'He's always strutting around in his smart clothes, thinking he's better than everyone else. You must be stupid to let someone like him join your village! I'll tell you what – I have a magic hoop. I'll throw it over him and he'll become helpless.'

Some of the young men of the village envied Rabbit Boy's power and popularity, and so they were easily persuaded to attack him. Then Iktome threw his hoop over the boy, who was actually unaffected but pretended to be powerless just to amuse himself.

The young men then tied Rabbit Boy to a tree with strong buffalo hide thongs. Rabbit Boy seemed unafraid, which annoyed them all the more. Iktome helped to stir them up and then, as if suddenly thinking of a good idea, he cried, 'Let's take our butchering knives and cut him to pieces!'

'Dear friends,' said Rabbit Boy calmly, 'if you're going to murder me, let me sing my death chant first.' Out of grudging respect, they waited while he sang his song, which told how he had fought the sun and won. The song done, they stabbed Rabbit Boy to death, sliced him up and put the meat in a cooking pot. But when they did this, a black cloud blotted out the sun and when it passed away the pot was empty. Those who had watched carefully had seen the pieces of meat reassemble themselves as the body of Rabbit Boy, which had then ridden up to the spirit world on a shaft of sunlight.

A wise elder said: 'Rabbit Boy has great power. When he returns from visiting the sun he'll be more powerful still. Let's make sure he marries the girl who loves him.'

Iktome was now incensed. 'Forget Rabbit Boy,' he shouted. 'I'm more powerful than him. Take my knife and cut me up, and see if I'm not!'

So they tied him up and he tried to remember the song that Rabbit Boy had sung – but he got it wrong, singing about the moon instead of the sun, and so when they cut him up and put his body in the pot, that's where it stayed.

COMMENTARY

There are many myths worldwide of heroes rising above humble circumstances. Starting life as a blood-clot kicked around by a rabbit clearly qualifies as 'humble', but this only serves to emphasize the hero's innate superiority over other men. However, there is in fact a natural power inherent in Rabbit Boy's origins. First, many tribes ascribe a special power to blood itself and for the Lakota it is the source of the world (see page 9). Then there is the power of movement, similar to the Navajo concept of *nilchi* or Holy Wind (see page 23). Third, in many myths, early adoption by animals puts the hero in touch with the life-force found in nature, which fuels his later achievements. Romulus and Remus are a case in point.

Many hero myths are also about initiation into manhood. 'Rabbit Boy' deals with initiation, not just into manhood, but into humanity. It is as if maturity involves coming out of the pre-human animal state into a fully human one. Yet Rabbit Boy is actually superhuman, as his vision of the sun shows early on. Heroes are frequently identified with the sun, but this myth goes a step further: Rabbit Boy proves himself superior to the sun. The girl, who slips out of the story before the end, is an anima figure who in other forms of the hero myth would be the hero's reward for overcoming obstacles.

Iktome is a classic trickster. (For his origins, see pages 10–11; for tricksters generally, Chapter 1.) Tricksters are often associated with the hero, playing the role of his Shadow. Just as the hero, through striving, makes the most of his assets, the trickster is often brought down by his lower nature. In this tale Iktome succumbs to envious spite. His mistake in singing about the moon – which only reflects the sun, rather than about the sun itself – underlines his inferiority to the solar hero.

Finally, Rabbit Boy's bodily resurrection testifies to the power of spirit, symbolized by the sunbeam on which he rides up to the spirit world. It also reverses the Fall: the scattered fragments into which nature has descended are restored to their primal unity.

The horse transformed life for the Plains tribes

11 | LONG ARROW AND THE ELK DOGS

This Blackfoot story tells how the tribe received their first horses, which they called elk dogs because they were at least as big as elks and replaced their dogs as pack animals. It is based on an account by ethnohistorian George Bird Grinnell given in about 1901.

A deaf boy and his beautiful sister one day lost both their parents at once and so had to fend for themselves. People liked the girl's looks and her pleasant manner and soon she was adopted by another family. As for the boy, however, no one wanted him. They thought he was stupid because he was deaf and could not understand what was said to him. He was beaten when he tried to warm himself at someone else's fire or when he hung around hoping to be given something to eat. He had to content himself with picking up odd scraps thrown out for the dogs and any berries he could find on bushes outside the village. His clothes became ragged and at night he huddled in a scrape in the ground, which he lined with grass. His life was little better than that of an animal.

The time came for the band to move camp. The tipis were taken down and packed up on sleds to be pulled by the dogs. The boy tried to follow, but the people told him to stay behind. 'We don't want a useless boy like you,' they said.

The orphan boy hung around for a while, scouring the area where the tipis had been standing, hoping to find some scraps to live on. After a few days, when the grass where the tipis had stood was just beginning to turn green again, the boy decided that his only chance was to follow his people. Weak and exhausted, he hurried after them as best he could, tears sometimes streaking his dirty face. Then something snapped in his right ear; a tiny worm came out and he could hear the song of the lark for the first time. The same happened with his left ear and at once he could hear the sound of a stream. Amazed and happy for the first time since his parents died, he stood taking in the sounds all around, then hurried on with new hope.

After a while he came to the new camp, where people were still settling in, putting up tipis and gathering firewood. Most of the men had gone out hunting, but an old chief, Good Running, was still in the camp, butchering a buffalo. The orphan boy caught his eye and he looked so tired and dirty that the old man took pity on him. 'Come on – sit and have some offal,' he said, beckoning the boy. The old man noticed that there was a change in the boy: even while cramming the meat into his mouth, he seemed more aware of what was going on than before. Good Running gave him a better piece of meat.

The kind old man began to take a liking to the boy. 'Grandson,' he said, 'you remind me of my own sons – all grown now. I'm going to adopt you and make a hunter and a warrior of you and make sure that people call you by your proper name – Long Arrow.'

When the old chief's wife heard of the plan, she was far from pleased. 'Why do you want to bring a burden like this on us? Can you hunt and fill an extra mouth at your age? And what about me – I have enough to do!'

But the chief was firm and his wife had to accept the newcomer, like it or not. Long Arrow began to learn to speak and he gradually caught up with other boys of his age. He could run like a deer and learned to hunt well. Even so, while no one insulted him to his face anymore, people remembered that he had once been an outcast, and they kept a distance from him.

One day Long Arrow went to the old chief. 'Grandfather,' he said, 'I want to do something for the tribe that will make you proud of me and earn me respect.'

'I'm proud of you already, grandson. And one day you'll become a chief like me and win the respect you deserve.'

'But I want to do something now! Is there nothing the people need that I could achieve?'

The old man thought. He was very fond of the boy now and depended on him. He had no desire to send him on a dangerous mission. Reluctantly, then, he said to the boy: 'Sometimes people speak of a distant lake. At the bottom of the lake is a land where spirit people live. They have great animals, the elk dogs, who do all their work for them. Now, if you were to journey to this land and bring back an elk dog, surely then the people would be astonished at the feat. They might even make you a chief right away!'

Long Arrow was determined to go and so the old man began to teach the boy the ways of manhood, so that he would be ready for this test of courage. Over a period of time the old chief taught him the prayers that men say. He also built a sweatlodge of willow branches and hides, and the boy was purified in its sage-scented steam. The elders made him a medicine and a shield with magical signs on it to protect him.

Then one dawn the old man provided the young man with a dog sled and a bow, saw him to the edge of the village, purified him with cedar smoke, and wished him luck.

Long Arrow headed south and after three days he came to a pond. Here the spirit of the pond, in the shape of a man, was waiting for him. The spirit directed him to continue for sixteen days or so until he came to a lake, where he should seek the help of another spirit man. The young man continued, rising before dawn and travelling on, hardly stopping for rest, wearing out his moccasins. He endured heat by day in the dry valleys and cold at night in the mountains. At length he came to a lake nestling between pine-covered hills. As he approached its edge, a fierce-looking giant of a man appeared, carrying a war-lance.

'Little man,' said the scowling stranger, 'what do you want here?'

'To find the elk dogs for my people,' said the young man.

The giant came up close to Long Arrow. 'Have you no fear of me?' he asked menacingly. His scowl turned to a crooked grin when he saw that Long Arrow was unafraid.

'Good,' said the stranger, his manner changing. 'Keep going south. If you're lucky, you may find my grandfather.' Then he vanished into the glassy lake.

Long Arrow carried on, through valleys and over high peaks, living on what he could hunt or gather from the bushes. He hardly slept or even rested and by the time he got into the high mountains, he was so exhausted that he could barely tell if what appeared to be a huge lake surrounded by snowy peaks was really there or had swum up from his own imagination. He collapsed and slept at last.

He was awoken by the chill of morning sinking into his bones and by the rattle of a porcupine bustling past. He rubbed his eyes and there before him was a beautiful boy in a white buckskin decorated with quills of every colour of the rainbow.

'We have been waiting for you, Long Arrow,' smiled the child. 'My grandfather has told me to invite you to our home. Come.'

At this the boy took the form of a kingfisher and dived into the lake. Long Arrow left his dog and sled behind, but took his shield and bow with him. Summoning his courage and thinking of the old chief, he dived in.

He was surprised and relieved to find that the water parted to let him through, and that in a few moments he found himself standing on the surface of another lake, which was in another land. He continued to a valley where stood a large tipi decorated with crimson images of animals whose like Long Arrow had never seen before. Then he caught sight of a flash of blue and then the beautiful boy stood before him smiling and gesturing towards the tipi's entrance.

Inside the tipi sat an old man in a long black robe, over which the white hair of many winters flowed. His eyes bored into Long Arrow, who could tell that this was a man of great power. The wise man's wife now brought food for Long Arrow, who was hungry after his journey. He remembered the time when Good Running had given him meat when no one else had a kind word for him. As he ate he looked around at the fine shields, bows and shirts hanging around the tipi.

Seeing his interest, the old man said, meaningfully, 'We will smoke the pipe and then I will think about giving you a gift to take back with you.'

They smoked, and then the old man said, 'Go with my grandson. He has something to show you.'

The beautiful boy took Long Arrow to a green valley. Long Arrow heard a drumming on the turf and heard an unfamiliar snorting sound. Then a great herd of big animals appeared, thundering towards him. They had long tails and the hair on their necks blew like streamers in the wind. Their feet were hooves and their long legs looked strong and muscular.

'What are these creatures?' asked Long Arrow, thinking that he already knew the answer.

'They are the elk dogs,' replied his companion. 'Let me show you how to ride them.' And he caught hold of one of the creatures, swung his body over it and set off at a gallop across the meadow.

Now Long Arrow tried, and as his feet gripped the elk dog's broad, glossy flanks, the animal raced off and Long Arrow felt like an eagle riding the wind.

After this, the beautiful boy spoke seriously to Long Arrow. 'I want you to have what you came for. This is what you must do. Try to catch a glimpse of my grandfather's feet beneath his robe. If you do, he will have to offer you whatever gift you want. Accept nothing but the mallard duck and her young.'

So they returned to the tipi. Long Arrow stayed there for three more days, during which time he watched closely. Then one day, the old man was leaving the tipi when his robe caught on a bow hanging near the entrance flap and was lifted slightly. Long Arrow at once saw the old man's secret. His feet were hooves!

Nodding as if he had been expecting this, the old man turned to Long Arrow. 'So – it was meant to be. Now you know my secret, what gift will you take back to your people?'

'The mallard duck and her young,' said Long Arrow quickly.

The old man laughed. 'You don't want her – she's old and losing her feathers. How about a magic medicine shield, or this fine bow with a string that can never break?'

But Long Arrow persisted.

'I see you are wise, young man,' said the old medicine man. 'Take your gift and go in peace to your people. The ducks will follow you. But be warned: don't look back until you're back in your own world.'

Long Arrow said farewell to the boy who had helped him, and to the old man. Then he returned to the lake, dived in, and in a few moments found himself being greeted by his dog, faithfully waiting by the sled. Now that he was back in his own world, he could look back. As he did, he saw a herd of elk dogs emerging in a shower of spray from the lake in place of the ducks. Rejoicing in his good fortune, he freed his dog from the sled and caught one of the animals to pull it instead. Then he mounted the finest beast, a black stallion, and led the herd back over the mountains to his people.

When he arrived, he went straight to Good Running, who was overjoyed to see him and astonished to see the elk dogs. The people were afraid of the animals at first, but Long Arrow taught them how to ride the elk dogs and use them to pull loads. He kept the black stallion for himself and gave the rest of the herd to the people.

'My grandson,' said Good Running, 'I am truly proud of you. Now all of the tribe will know the name of Long Arrow.'

The tribe made Long Arrow a chief. The Blackfoot became skilled riders and soon wondered how they had ever managed to live without the elk dogs.

COMMENTARY

This story is especially interesting in that it stands at the point where a historical event has evolved into a legend and then a fully fledged myth. In the seventeenth and eighteenth centuries the Plains became very unsettled socially as tribes gradually acquired two things that had a drastic effect on their lifestyle and especially on their hunting and military tactics. These two things were firearms and horses. The latter were probably never indigenous to North America; if they ever were in prehistoric times, then they had certainly died out long before the Spanish introduced their own horses, which escaped and bred in the wild. Some tribes acquired firearms first, others horses, and there are some reports of confused confrontations between tribes that had one and not the other.

Before the tribes had horses, they used dog sleds for pulling loads. There was buffalo hunting, but it depended on stealthy hunters creeping up on the buffalo or driving them over cliffs. The

Cheyenne's horses were to become indispensable to them both in the hunt and in battle.

The poor boy hero

Like so many heroes, Long Arrow is poor and orphaned. He is particularly unlucky in that his sister is adopted and he is not (she then fades from the story), and in his deafness, which is taken for stupidity. One could read symbolic meaning into this deafness, but there is no real need for this: it is just an affliction which comes to an end. It does, however, mean that when he mysteriously regains his hearing, he has a fresh start.

He is lucky in being taken under the wing of the kindly Good Running, whose faith in the boy and unconditional love for him (contrasting with the attitude of the tribe and even at first of Good Running's wife) give Long Arrow the strength to make something of himself. This discovery by the hero of a benign father-figure, as opposed to one who sets tests, is relatively unusual. In many hero myths a father-figure is responsible for sending the young hero off on an initiatory quest. Here, however, that role is played by the tribe's continued prejudice towards the boy. However, Good Running does initiate Long Arrow into the rites of manhood.

The quest

Long Arrow faces a test of courage and endurance in his long journey. It is also a test of his spiritual power, however, as is shown by the gradual ascent into the mountains, the increasing size of the lakes and his encounters with their spirits. These spirits are guardians of the threshold. Their purpose is to deter the spiritual seeker who is not yet ready for an encounter with the divine. When they discover that Long Arrow is unafraid, they know that he is ready.

The pond and the lakes relate, of course, to the unconscious. As in the image of the cloud on the mountain found in the birth of Changing Woman, the mountain lake symbolizes access to the spiritual realm through the unconscious. The third spirit, the beautiful boy, in Jungian terms represents the inner self of the seeker, who is very much in contrast with our earlier image of the dirty, neglected orphan. He invites Long Arrow to face a vital test – the test of faith, which he must have in order to plunge into the lake, or the unconscious, overcoming the fear of drowning, or ego loss. The image of the lake as a portal through the unconscious to the world of the spirit is found in the myths of many cultures, in particular the Celtic. Interestingly, there are also Celtic myths (for example of Cuchulainn) in which horses come from lakes.

The fulfilment

In the watery spirit world, Long Arrow encounters the archetype of the Wise Old Man. In a sense this man is a spiritual counterpart of Good Running. Both have Long Arrow's interests at heart, although the Wise Old Man also tests his motives and does not simply bestow gifts upon the seeker without a trial. The old man is, of course, linked to the horses by his hooves. This indicates the strong Native American belief in the idea that a human being can partake of the power of an animal with whom he (or less often she) has a particular affinity. Long Arrow is helped to achieve his quest by the beautiful boy, who has now become a 'magical helper' figure. A final test of faith is involved in Long Arrow following his advice to ask for the ducks.

Having secured his goal, Long Arrow can return to his own world. Back on the lake shore he finds his dog waiting for him. The dog is a symbol of loyalty and would be associated by the Cheyenne with the Dog Men warrior society (see page 40). It also relates to the part of the psyche that has waited patiently for the shaman's return from the potentially dangerous realm of the unconscious.

Returning to his tribe, Long Arrow at last gains the respect that he deserves. However, he would not be a true hero without a final act of altruism – giving all but one of the horses to the tribe.

12 | THE MEDICINE GRIZZLY BEAR

This Pawnee tale is adapted from a longer version by George Bird Grinnell, first published in *Harper's Monthly*, 1901.

There was once a poor boy whose father had been an important man in the tribe before losing his luck. When the man went hunting he brought back nothing, when he fought he achieved nothing and the people no longer respected him. But his son had a friend, a chief's son who loved the poor boy, and these two were like brothers. They hunted together and went courting together; the poor boy often rode one of the ponies of the chief's son, and the chief's son often used to sleep at the poor boy's lodge.

One day the camp went off to hunt buffalo and the boys rode together all the time. After the people had made camp, the chiefs decided to stop there for a while, because the buffalo were plentiful. North of the camp was a hill topped with cedars, and the poor boy heard it said that it was a dangerous place, where many people had died. Hearing this, the poor boy thought about how poor he and his father were, and how everybody looked down on them, and he made up his mind to go up into those cedars.

He went out of the lodge and started to go towards the trees. The moon was bright, so he could see well. Just before he reached the edge of the timber he saw that the ground was white with human bones. Nevertheless he went on into the cedars and came to a ravine and followed it up the hill. When he came to the head of the ravine, there was a cave in the bank, with a worn path leading into it. He hesitated for a moment, but then went in. And when his eyes had become accustomed to the dark, he saw there, sitting by the fire, a big she-bear and her cubs.

The she-bear said to him: 'You should never have come here. My husband will kill you and feed you to us if he sees you! He's gone hunting, but he'll be back soon.'

The poor boy said: 'I came here to die and I give myself up to feed you. Take me.'

As if ignoring his words, the she-bear said: 'Listen: when you hear a noise outside, pick up that cub, the smallest one and hold it in your arms. When my husband comes in, he'll tell you to put it down, but don't.'

At once the boy heard the noise of a bear snorting and grunting outside the cave. The she-bear said: 'Quick, pick up the cub – he's coming.' The boy caught up the cub and held it tight. The noise outside stopped at the mouth of the den. It was the Bear. The boy could hear him talking. He said: 'Hah! Someone has been around my house. I smell a human. Where is he?' When he came in and saw the boy, he seemed furious. He stood up on his hind feet and threw up his front paws and then came down again and struck the cave floor. Then he reared up and snorted red dust from his nostrils and then came down and made rushes towards the boy as if to seize him. The boy was afraid but stood his ground.

The Bear roared, 'How dare you touch my child! Let go, or I'll tear you to pieces.' But no matter what the Bear said or did, the boy held fast to the cub.

When the Bear saw this, he became quiet and no longer seemed angry. Instead, he said: 'Human boy, you are now my son. Put down my cub, for he is now your brother. He will be your companion, guide and helper. He's told me about your unhappiness and now he's saved you. I have taken pity on you and we will send you back to your people, where you may do some good among them. I am head of all the animal lodges; there is no animal living that is stronger than me. I can make arrows fall from my skin without hurting me. Look up around my lodge at the weapons that foolish men have brought, thinking to kill me.'

'Now, my son, all the power that I have I give to you. I shall kill my son, your little brother there, and give you his skin to keep. Your brother at the camp is looking for you, but tomorrow night you'll see him and tell him where you've been.'

The cub said to the boy: 'It's all right now, brother; put me down. Trust my father. I am glad that I am going to be with you.' So the boy put him down.

Then the Bear and his wife walked around the fire in a circle and sang and the boy looked on. The Bear took a gun and, to the boy's surprise, he shot the she-bear dead. Then he put his mouth on her wound and breathed on it and snorted, and sucked the bullet out. In a moment she had come back to life. Then he did the same to the boy, who was amazed and relieved to find himself still alive.

Then he handed over the gun and invited the boy to shoot him. Still doubtful, the boy did as he was told. The Bear fell over, but after a moment he got to his feet and slapped his paws on his chest several times, and the bullet came out. He walked around the fireplace two or three times, made motions and grunted, and then he was well again. Then he took the boy in his arms and breathed on him, and said: 'Now I give you my power. I will shoot you again as you shot me. This time, do just as I did.' The boy allowed himself to be shot, and when he did just as the Bear had done, he found that he had healed himself.

The Bear then demonstrated the same power with a bow and arrow. Finally, he said: 'You see, my son. Nothing can harm me and you now have this power as well. When you go into battle, take no gun or bow. Instead, cover your body with this red paint, tie this feather in your hair and take this club, which is a part of my jawbone. These things will protect you and give you power over your enemy.'

The next morning the Bear took the boy out on the prairie and showed him the different roots and leaves of medicines and told him how to use them, eating some of the medicine and effecting a cure by just breathing on the wound.

The Bear said to him: 'From now on you will have the same feelings as a bear. When you get angry, you'll grunt like a bear; and if you feel fierce, your teeth will become sharp like a bear's teeth, so that the people will know that you're angry.'

The Bear took the claw from his little finger and gave it and a little bundle of medicine to the boy. He said: 'Take this claw and this medicine bundle. Put them on a string and wear them on your neck always, the claw hanging in front.' The Bear then taught him how to make plums grow on trees and how to make ground-cherries come out of his mouth.

That night he sent the boy back to the camp to fetch tobacco and a pipe. While there, the boy smoked with his friend the chief's son, but then he returned to the bear family, filled his pipe and smoked with the Bear. Then the Bear said to him: 'After you have gone home, whenever you smoke, always point your pipe towards my den and ask me to smoke with you. After lighting your pipe, point it first to the Great Spirit and then blow some smoke to me. Then I shall know that you still remember me. So long as I live I will protect you; when I die, you will die too.'

After this he said, 'Now bring my youngest boy here.' The boy brought the little cub and the Bear said: 'Now kill him.' The boy hesitated to do this, but the cub said, 'Go on, my brother, kill me. After this I will be a spirit and I will always be with you.' So the boy killed him, tanned his hide and painted it with red medicine paint. The Bear next told him to put his paint, feathers and war-club in this hide and to make a bundle of them and hang them in his lodge at home, keeping it secret from the tribe.

When the boy reached home, the people were surprised to see him again, but soon forgot about his absence. But then the boy told the chief's son that he wanted him to go off with him on the warpath. They went, the poor boy taking his bundle. After many days they came to an enemy camp and made off with a string of horses. The enemy pursued them, but the poor boy quickly dismounted, telling his brother to go on with the horses.

The boy had painted himself red. He held his war-club in his hand and had his feather tied on his head and the bearskin on his back. The enemy attacked, but they could not harm him. When they saw this, they backed away, realizing that he had great power. When he caught up with the chief's son, he too realized what power the boy now had and when they returned he told the rest of the village about it.

A few days after they reached home a war-party attacked the village. All the Pawnees went out to fight, but the poor boy stayed in his lodge. He took down his bundle, filled the pipe and smoked it as he had been taught to do. Then he painted his body red and his face black, put the feather on his head and the little bear-robe on his back, and took his war-club in his hand and went into battle, attacking from the east.

As he came up he saw that there was one of the enemy who seemed to be the bravest of all. The poor boy rushed at this man and killed him, and then ran back to his own line. When his people saw that the poor boy had done this brave deed, they knew that he really did have power and they followed him. He ran among the enemy, wreaking havoc with his club. That night the Pawnees returned to the village, rejoicing over the victory. Women danced before the poor boy and men sang his praises.

The Bear had told him that when he wanted his name changed he must call himself Medicine Bear, so this is the name that the poor boy now took.

That night the Bear came to the boy in his sleep and spoke to him. He said: 'My son, tomorrow your chief will ask you to marry his daughter, but you must not do this yet. There are things that you must do first. If you take a wife now, your power will leave you.'

The next day the chief came to Medicine Bear, offered him his daughter, and told him the people wanted him to be their head chief. But Medicine Bear refused.

Some time after this all the different tribes that had been attacked by him joined forces and came down together to fight the Pawnees. All the people went out to meet them, but Medicine Bear stayed in his lodge and prepared himself as always. When he came to the battle, he charged in and killed a man and then came back, and the second time he charged, the people followed him and they won another victory. Everybody rejoiced and there were many scalp dances. Now the poor boy was more highly thought of than ever. Even the chiefs bowed their heads when they saw him.

One day the head chief said: 'Medicine Bear, in all this tribe there is no chief equal to you. Sit by my daughter. Take her to wife and take my place as chief. My lodge is yours.'

But the boy was not yet ready to do this. The girl was very pretty and he liked her, but he felt that before he married there were still things he must do. He called his brother and said to him: 'Go, kill a fat buffalo; bring it to me and we will go on a long journey.'

His brother killed a buffalo and brought the meat home, and they dried it and made a bundle of it. Medicine Bear told his brother to carry this bundle and a rawhide rope and a hatchet, and they started out. One evening they reached the river and found themselves on top of a steep-cut bluff above the Missouri River. The poor boy cut a cottonwood pole and drove it into the ground. He tied the rope to it and then tied the other end round his brother's body. Then he sharpened a stick and gave it to his brother, saying: 'Now take the bundle of meat and I will lower you over the bank. Put the meat on a ledge and when the birds come you must feed them. They are the ones that have power and they can take pity on you.' So he let the chief's son down.

The first bird that came was a buzzard, then an eagle, then hawks and owls, all kinds of birds that kill their prey. The chief's son fed them all. Meanwhile Medicine Bear lay on top of the bank. Just as the sun was going down, he saw, far up the river, a flock of geese. They came nearer and at last passed out of sight. After, when he looked down on the river, it seemed to be on fire and he could hear below him the sound of drumming and singing. And all the time the chief's son was hanging below, feeding the birds. Eventually, Medicine Bear started for home, leaving the chief's son hanging there.

The chief's son stayed there for three days and nights, and on the fourth night he fell asleep. When he awoke he was in a lodge under the Missouri River. When he looked about him he saw that those in the lodge were all animals. Every kind of animal was there. Then, one by one, each of the animals gave the chief's son its special medicine power to protect and heal, to kill enemies, to see by night like the owl and to run swiftly like the deer. They told him that at this time they could teach him only a little, but that later they would meet him out on the prairie and teach him more. At last they said: 'Now it is time for you to go. Your friend has come and he's waiting for you out on the prairie.'

The Buffalo now stood up and said: 'My son, I want to be with you always. I give you my robe. Wear it wherever you go, that the people may know that you come from this place.' All the animals then added something to the robe – a feather, a claw, or some sweet grass. Then they said, 'Go, my son, to your people and bring us something to smoke.'

Presently the chief's son found himself upon the bluff, facing his brother. Medicine Bear grasped him in his arms and said: 'Oh, my brother, what a fine robe you have on!' Then they went home together.

Soon after this the Pawnees had a big doctors' dance. The two young men went and demonstrated their powers and the chief's son was chosen to be the head doctor. When the dance was over, the two brothers at once started to go to the animals' lodge, carrying with them tobacco and a pipe. When they got there, the chief's son told his brother to wait on the bank, because he was going down to take the tobacco and the pipe to his fathers. He jumped off the steep bank into the river, down into the door of the lodge, and went in. When they saw him all the animals slapped their mouths and called out. They were glad to see him. After smoking with them, he went back to his friend. After that the chief's son would go off by himself and would meet the animals on the hills. They would tell him about different roots and how to cure diseases.

Finally the head chief sent for Medicine Bear and said: 'My son, I offered you my lodge, my daughter and the tribe. Now take all this.' The young man said: 'What of my brother? Send for the other chief. Let him give his daughter, his lodge, his people to him and this day we will accept your gifts to us. My brother will after this be the head doctor of this tribe.' The other chief agreed and it was done.

Medicine Bear went on the warpath often, but his brother stayed at home and fought the enemy only when they attacked the village. He took charge of the doctors' lodge. Medicine Bear had children and when they had grown up he told his son the secrets of his power. He was now growing old and his son went on the warpath, while he remained in camp.

One night Medicine Bear had a dream about his Bear father. The Bear said to him: 'My son, I made you powerful among your people. But now my coat is growing thin and soon I shall die. Then you too will die. Tell your son all the secret powers that I gave you. Now they will be his.'

Soon after this the old bear died and so did Medicine Bear. But before he died he said to his brother: 'Don't mourn for me. I will always be near you. Take care of your people. Cure them when they're sick and always be their chief.'

For as long as he lived, the chief's son remembered these words and did his best for the people.

COMMENTARY

This tale reflects the Native American attitude towards animals and their powers, and the relationship between the natural and spirit worlds. The Pawnee had secret societies dedicated to animal spirits. Every animal was thought to have its own particular powers, and one of the special powers of the grizzly bear, demonstrated here, was healing. The Native view is that behind, or within, the individual animal is the essence of the species. In Jungian terms the grizzly in this story embodies the grizzly archetype, with all its magical powers.

The hero's encounter

The boy who is to become Medicine Bear is typical of the hero whose poor start in life forces him to forge his own destiny. In particular, his father is poor, unlucky and not respected in the tribe. In fact he has such a low profile in the story that he quickly drops out of it altogether. Therefore in a sense when the boy meets the grizzly he is going through the familiar hero's encounter with the father, with its attendant dangers, tests and eventual rewards. This takes place when the boy's despair has brought him to the point of throwing his life away. He is unafraid of death, as the hero must be when he meets the father. However, the encounter takes place in a cave, the symbolic womb of the earth, and in taking the she-bear's advice he is following another part of the hero pattern: he is like Theseus accepting the ball of twine from Ariadne before entering the labyrinth to confront the Minotaur.

In the Navajo myth, when t.
appears to be savagely angry a
when satisfied that the boys are
the Bear just as quickly loses his
has shown himself to be brave an

The spirit path

A different kind of bravery is ne
instructions and kill the bear cub. Here
belief in the enduring power of the s⟩ ...ectly
content to die, knowing that he will beco⟩ ...ielong spirit
helper. The Bear's elaborate demonstrati⟩ ...nis ability to make
himself immune to bullets and arrows is also far from fanciful.
Most tribes believed in the power of magic and personal spirit
power to protect an individual from harm. This was the basis of the
belief in the painted 'ghost shirts' worn by the Ghost Dancers.
Although it did not always work, a persuasive account of this
power is given by Black Elk in *Black Elk Speaks*. He describes
riding unharmed through a hail of cavalry bullets.

It is important that the boy follows the Bear's instructions correctly
when he goes into battle. He paints himself in red (for holiness) and
black (for death) and approaches the battlefield from the correct
direction – that of the rising sun. Through being adopted by the
Bear, and by following these instructions, he gains the Bear's
powers. It is also important that he shows respect to his bear father
by bringing him a pipe and tobacco and by continuing to honour
him when he smokes the pipe. The Pawnee attitude to the pipe was
similar to that of the Lakota (see page 45). Lastly, the boy obeys the
instructions for preparing and keeping his secret medicine bundle.

Among his own people, Medicine Bear wins respect not just by his
achievements on the battlefield, but by the spiritual power that
makes them possible, which he has gained from his bear father. (It
is interesting, too, that the spiritual path is not seen as being at odds
with making war on other tribes.) However, the chief's son is to
achieve even greater powers. Initially it is Medicine Bear who
starts the chief's son on this path. This is fitting, since the two are
almost inseparable. Many tribes had, and still have even today, a

friends could formally seal their friendship. … was the Hunka ceremony.) By taking part in …y were undertaking a lifelong commitment to help … It seems that this is the kind of friendship that the …on and Medicine Bear have. Hence Medicine Bear sets up …riend's gruelling shamanistic experience dangling from the cliff overlooking the Missouri. The reference to the birds taking pity on him relates to the idea that spirits could take pity on humans and grant them visions from which they would gain spiritual power. The chief's son has a spectacular vision, by which he obtains the special powers, especially healing powers, of all the animals.

It is also interesting that Medicine Bear defers marriage until he has completed his spiritual and magical apprenticeship. He puts his spiritual path, and what he seems to regard as his destiny, before the more mundane demands of family life. At the same time, he does eventually take up his social obligation to marry, produce children and become a leader of his tribal group.

Iroquois false-face mask

13 | THE POWERFUL BOY

This Seneca tale is based on an account recorded by J. Curtin and J. Hewitt in about 1910.

A couple lived with their young son in a lodge in the forest. The woman became pregnant but to the great sorrow of her husband, she died in childbirth, even though the baby was tiny – no bigger than a hand. The man assumed that the tiny boy would die and so he wrapped the baby up and placed it in a hollow tree.

The father had to go hunting every day to provide for himself and his surviving son, and so the boy was left on his own. Bored and lonely, he was sitting by the lodge when he heard a sound coming from the hollow tree. When he investigated, he found his tiny brother, who was alive and well – but hungry. The boy made some soup for them both, and when the tiny boy had drunk it, he was strong enough to scamper around. The boy was delighted and made his new brother a little deerskin coat.

When the father came home, he noticed some tiny tracks around the fire, and the older boy confessed that he had rescued the tiny boy from the tree, but that the child had now hidden himself.

'We'll tempt him out,' said the man. 'Go and invite him to hunt mice with you in an old tree stump.' Then the man caught some mice, hid them about himself and squatted down looking like an old tree stump.

The tiny boy was tempted out and the two boys had great fun racing around and catching mice – which to the tiny boy seemed as big as deer did to anyone else. Suddenly the stump grew a hand and grabbed the tiny boy, who wriggled in fear, but could not escape.

The tiny boy screamed, until the man put a little club in his hand to quieten him. Intrigued by this new toy, the infant whirled it around and then went and hit a tree with it. The tree split and fell to the ground in a great crash that sent birds squawking into the sky. It was the same with everything he hit: it was instantly destroyed.

Next time the father went to hunt, he said to his sons, 'While I'm away, don't go to the north. It's dangerous there.'

But as soon as the father was gone, the tiny boy said, 'Come on – let's go north.' He persuaded his brother and off they went. After a while they heard frogs croaking, but it sounded like people calling for their father. The tiny boy thought that someone wished his father harm and he gathered up stones and killed the frogs.

When they got home the father was angry to hear where they had been. 'Don't ever go there again,' he said. 'And what's more, don't go west either; that's just as bad.'

However, the next day as soon as the father had left the camp, the tiny boy urged his brother to accompany him on an expedition to the west to see what was there. The boys travelled west, until they came to a tall pine tree with what looked like a platform and a bed on top.

'I wonder what's up there,' said the tiny boy and immediately started to climb up. He found two naked babies up there and on seeing him the children started to call for their father. Soon there was a great rumbling sound and a Thunder Being appeared in the branches of the tree. But before he could do a thing, the tiny boy hit him over the head with his little club and left him dead.

Then the children began to call for their mother and in a moment another huge Thunder Being appeared – and was dispatched in the same way as the first. The tiny boy looked at the babies and thought their skin would make a good tobacco pouch for his father, so he killed them both. Then the boys went home.

Once again, their father was angry. 'Why did you kill the Thunder babies?' he demanded incredulously. 'Their parents brought us rain, but now they'll seek revenge.'

'I've killed them all,' said the tiny boy. So, still grumbling, the father took the skins for a pouch. But he added, 'You may have come to no harm so far, but don't ever go to the north again – because that's where the giant Stone Coat lives.'

'Stone Coat?' thought the tiny boy. 'I wonder wha⌐

The next day the tiny boy tried to persuade his bro⌐ north, but this time the brother thought he had bette⌐ father. The tiny boy set off alone through the woods. A⌐ time, he heard the sound of a huge dog barking. It belo⌐ ⌐u to Stone Coat. Hearing the dog coming closer, the boy jumped into a chestnut tree to hide. The dog came bounding up, followed by its owner. When the dog kept barking at the tree, Stone Coat hit it with his huge club and out fell the tiny boy.

The giant bent down and peered at him closely. 'What a tiny creature you are!' said Stone Coat. 'Don't you get enough to eat?'

'Perhaps that's it,', said the boy, as he ran along beside the giant.

Stone Coat had a bear in each pocket, and when they got to the camp, he said: 'Come on, we'll fatten you up. I'll eat one bear, you eat the other.'

'Fine,' said the boy. 'Can I kill you if I finish mine first?'

'Certainly,' said the giant, amused at the idea.

The boy cut up his bear and appeared to be eating it, but he kept running outside and hiding the meat. Finally he said, 'There. I've finished, and you haven't. Can I kill you now?'

'First let me show you how to slide downhill – you'll enjoy it.'

The giant took the boy and put him in a bowl and pushed it hard down a steep grassy bank with a cave at the bottom. A few minutes later, he was surprised to see the boy return. 'What's next?' asked the boy enthusiastically.

'Mm ... We'll try log kicking. Let's see who can kick this one higher.'

Stone Coat kicked the log into the sky. When it crashed back down, the boy tried and the log disappeared from view. Stone Coat was looking up for it, puzzled, when a tiny speck in the blue grew bigger and then turned into the log – which landed on him and crushed his skull.

That evening, the boy arrived home on Stone Coat's dog, which he gave to his father as a gift. The father was worried that Stone Coat would come to kill them, but was reassured by the tiny boy. 'Well, all right,' he said. 'But listen: whatever you do, don't go south-west.'

So next day the tiny boy went to the south-west, and when he got there he found a man with a huge head sitting and playing dice with other men. He always won, and as soon as he had a nice collection of defeated players, he cut their heads off. When those still waiting to play saw the boy, their hopes were raised, small though he was. The boy took his place by the big-headed man and they played. The boy's dice turned into woodcocks and flew up, then all landed the same side up, so that the boy won every throw – and claimed the gambling man's head as forfeit. The delighted people invited the boy to be their chief, but he said he would ask his father to be chief in his place.

The boy returned home, but the father had no desire to move to the south-west. The next day the boy went – as always, against his father's wishes – to the east. Here the Wolf and Bear clans were fighting the Eagle, Turtle and Beaver clans. The boy sided with the Wolf and the Bear; he led a great victory and won all the beautiful country of the east.

At last he went home and invited his father to be chief of this country. His father was pleased and agreed. He packed up the tipi and took his boys to live in the new country.

COMMENTARY

Like so many Native American myths, this one is only partly explanatory. Its ending gives a reason for the Seneca's migration across the continent to their homeland in the east. The war between the clans (which in another version is a game) may even be based on real events. The clans are real ones that survive to this day. However, the earlier part of the story is definitely myth rather than legend or rationalization.

The tiny boy is a type of the omnipotent infant, who is found all across the world. Hermes shows similar precocity and mischievous disobedience when he steals the cattle of Apollo and hides them in a cave. The tiny boy, in his diminutive stature and mighty deeds, resembles Tom Thumb, who is born to an old couple who wish for a son, and goes on to become a knight at the court of King Arthur. (This English folktale, recorded as early as 1597, was later collected by the brothers Grimm.) The type relates to the phase of human development when the infant believes himself to be all-powerful and all-important, before coming to perceive himself as separate from the world. It may also describe the power that a baby can have over its parents. More broadly speaking, it celebrates the heroic aspect of the human spirit that is prepared to do battle against the odds and to challenge paternal restrictions.

As in many tales, although not in actual Native American life, the small family is socially isolated. The death of the mother underlines the power of the boy, partly because his birth kills her, but also because he has no restraining or containing maternal influence. The father's placing of the baby inside a hollow tree perhaps echoes the ancient Greek practice of exposing a baby on a mountain top: it gets rid of an unwanted or handicapped child without actually killing it, and returns it to nature. Given this early start to life, it is interesting that the tiny boy later jumps into a tree to hide from Stone Coat.

The story includes the technique of repetition frequently used in folktales and especially in Native American tales, with the boy repeatedly being told not to go in a certain direction and the next day heading off in precisely that direction. It is almost as if the father, by forbidding something, is actually sending him on the quest. The first episode is unexceptional, but in the next the tiny boy behaves outrageously. His audacious slaughter of the Thunder Beings' babies is provocative in the extreme. It also demonstrates the naivety that is part of his power: the Thunder Beings are so powerful that normally no one would even think of challenging them. They are the spirits of the west, one of the great powers of the Four Directions. The episode also shows a rather playful and irreligious side to Native American belief: in these myths, even great gods can be made to look foolish or be killed off and then brought back to life in another story.

The time comes when the older brother fades out of the story and the focus is entirely on the tiny boy. This is the cue for his principal adventure, the encounter with Stone Coat. This giant's name probably refers to his being impervious to harm; it may also be that he was originally a mountain, perhaps in the Adirondack Range or the Green Mountains. (A similar metamorphosis may account for the Cyclops encountered by Odysseus in Sicily.) Stone Coat is in other ways like many ogres, especially those who set tests for young men. Often, as in the Welsh story of Cullwch and Olwen, the hero is competing for the hand of the ogre's daughter. Here, however, the boy competes out of pure childish enthusiasm.

The first test, the eating contest, echoes a fairly common folktale theme. Stith Thompson (*The Folktale*) even identifies a category of tale which he terms 'Eating contest won by deception', in which one common method of cheating is a bottomless bag. In a tale from the opposite corner of North America, in which the Hopi hero Son of Light fights Man Eagle, the latter challenges the hero to eating and smoking contests. The powerful boy uses his intelligence to make up for his size. Ogres are usually portrayed as physically strong but stupid, or at least possessing only a low cunning. The boy's victory champions the power of intelligence over physical strength and of creative ingenuity over the negative, life-denying aspect of the ego. We are not told how exactly the boy avoids death in his next test, in which the bowl hints at his becoming a snack for Stone Coat, and the cave a return to the womb of Mother Earth. In the final contest, with the log, the boy uses both strength and ingenuity.

The big-headed gambler seems to represent either fate or death – although there may also have been an actual tribe whose gambling suggested this figure. The boy's method of winning against him is connected to divination by the observation of bird flight: the implication is that by magically influencing the physical omen, one can influence the future event that it would normally be thought to predict.

It is interesting that the tiny boy, although repeatedly disobeying his father, always honours him: he kills the frogs, thinking they are a threat to his father; he gives his father the baby Thunder Being's skin for a tobacco pouch; he offers him the chiefdom of the 'gambling country'; and then finally he presents him with the beautiful land in the east. This honouring provides a balance to the boy's chaotic power and spontaneity, and the story's ending represents a return to the social order on which tribal life depends.

14 SAPANA – THE GIRL WHO CLIMBED TO THE SKY

This is an adaptation of a well-known Arapaho story. Similar tales exist among other Northern Plains tribes, including the Lakota and the Ojibway.

Sapana was the most beautiful young woman in her village and many young men wanted to marry her. But she was also hard-working, and so one morning she went with friends to gather firewood some distance outside the circle of her band's tipis. As they set about their task, Sapana heard a rattle of quills and looked round to see a large porcupine sitting watching her from the foot of a high cottonwood tree.

'Hey!' she called to the others. 'Help me to catch this fine porcupine and I'll divide its quills among you for our moccasins.'

As Sapana approached, the porcupine started to climb the tree. 'Quick,' she called to her friends, 'it's getting away.' And she started to climb after it as fast as she could. The porcupine stopped and looked round at her, but every time she thought she was about to catch up, it climbed higher.

'Come down, Sapana,' called a voice far below, but Sapana was determined – although the cottonwood seemed to go on for ever. When the very top of the tree was in sight, with the porcupine still just ahead of her, she saw what looked like a shining wall, and as the porcupine stepped off into it, she realized this must be the sky. When she looked down, her friends were tiny specks below and she felt she had no choice but to go on. So she followed the porcupine through the sky hole and found herself in a strange camp.

The porcupine now transformed himself into a rather ugly old man. Sapana was afraid, but the porcupine-man spoke gently to her and took her to his tipi to meet his parents. 'I've watched you,' he said. 'You're a good worker, as well as being beautiful – and there's plenty of work to do up here. I want you for my wife.'

With this, he set her to work preparing buffalo robes. It was hard and she missed her people. Each day the porcupine-man went off to hunt, returning with more buffalo hides for her to prepare. One day he told her she must go and dig for wild turnips. 'But be warned,' he added. 'Don't dig too deep.'

Sapana wondered why not, but after a while she forgot about this. She found a place where plenty of wild turnips grew and started to exercise her digging stick, putting the turnips into a skin bag on her side. Then she looked up and there was a huge turnip, with bushy green foliage sprouting out of it. 'This one will fill my bag,' she thought and she began to dig. The roots went far down, so that when she finally pulled the turnip out, a gaping hole appeared, so big that she almost fell through. She looked into it and her heart beat fast. There, far down below, was her own village, in her own world. She felt homesick and wished she could think of a way to get down.

Then she had an idea. First she replaced the huge turnip. Then she went back to her usual work of scraping and stretching buffalo hides. But she put aside the sinew where it would not be found. Every day she did this until she had enough to make a long rope. When the porcupine-man was out hunting, she wove a rope and then when she thought it was long enough, she coiled it up and took it to the turnip hole.

Sapana pulled the huge turnip out of the hole and tied one end of the rope to her digging stick, which she braced across the hole. She dropped the rest of the rope through the hole and into the clouds below. Then she wrapped a turn of the rope around herself and quickly began to climb down. The climb was long and her arms ached terribly. When she finally dared to look down, her heart leapt. She could see the treetops below her and the smoke from her people's tipis. 'Not far,' she told herself. But then her legs suddenly swung free of the rope and she was clinging on with her hands. It was too short!

Then the rope began to jerk about. A voice boomed down. 'Get back up here now or I'll shake you off!' It was the porcupine-man.

Sapana thought she was doomed. But then a spotted eagle flew past. 'Help me!' called the girl. The eagle obliged, hanging in the air while she climbed onto his back. He glided down, but after a while the effort was too much for him and it looked as if Sapana would fall.

Then a buzzard flew past. 'Climb on,' it said. The eagle flew off to rest and the buzzard continued down with Sapana. But soon the buzzard could go on no more. Then a hawk rose up beside them, hovering on flickering wings.

'Climb on,' said the hawk. The tipis were now in sight. Sapana did as she was told and the bird flew down and down, finally depositing her safely in her village.

Sapana thanked the hawk and lay exhausted on the ground. Then she stood and walked slowly towards her parents' tipi. On the way, a girl came towards her. It was Sapana's sister, who was amazed and joyful to see her.

Everyone was pleased to see Sapana again and eager to hear her story. And after this, whenever the people killed buffalo, they left one for the birds that had helped Sapana get back to earth.

COMMENTARY

In most Native American myths the spirit world is pictured as being in the sky. Sometimes, as in 'Long Arrow and the Elk Dogs', it is reached through a lake, but this is usually a mountain lake. There are a number of myths, especially among Plains tribes, which explore the relationship between this spirit world and the material world. There are strong indications that these myths are at least partly about reincarnation and what causes it.

Variations on a theme

Several of these myths involve young women who visit the sky world, become homesick and climb down a rope to earth, but then find themselves stranded in mid-air when the rope proves to be too short. The similarities and differences between these stories are revealing, so it is worth comparing the Arapaho myth with two other examples.

The Foolish Girls

In this Ojibway story, two young women want to sleep with stars, convinced that they will be wonderful lovers. They go to sleep and find their wish has come true: they have been transported to the spirit world and now have star husbands. But one complains that her virile young star husband wants sex too often, the other that her old fading one can hardly manage it at all. So they decide to escape. An old woman (called simply 'Old Woman') who guards a hole in the sky lets them look through it and glimpse their village (which in the spirit world is beneath them). She also gives them fibres from which to make a rope to lower down. They make their escape but the rope is too short and they get stuck in an eagle's nest. They call on a bear, a buffalo, a coyote and then a wolverine to get them down, tempting them with sexual favours. Finally, Wolverine gets them down.

Unfortunately Wolverine always makes love to them and then carries them back up the tree to the eagle's nest. Then Wolverine Woman comes along and they tell her that if she gets them down she can have the 'handsome' Wolverine Man, who returns and doesn't notice the difference until dawn. The two wolverines are shocked to find who their partner is, but decide they had better stay together because no one else would have them!

The Birth of Fallen Star

Two young Lakota women are star-gazing one night and wish they could marry stars. Suddenly they find themselves in the star world and they become the wives of two stars. They both become pregnant and are told not to dig any wild turnips. Of course one of them does, however, and this makes a hole through which she sees her village. Homesick, she braids turnip fibres to make a rope and climbs down. The rope is too short and she falls. She dies, but her baby is born, raised by a meadowlark, and becomes the Lakota culture hero Fallen Star.

Comparisons

All three stories begin with aspirations. In the Arapaho myth the young woman climbs in pursuit of the porcupine; in the other two the pairs of young women are carried up by wishful thinking. The transition to the spirit world signifies that they have died. The next point in common is that none of the young women is happy in the sky world; they all get homesick and want to return. Then there is the hole in the floor of the sky through which they glimpse their homeland. In the Arapaho and Lakota myths it is made by digging wild turnips. By doing this the young women are returning to the womb of Mother Earth (albeit in the sky). The old woman who guards the hole in the Lakota myth is Maya Owichapaha ('She who pushes them over the bank') and in Lakota belief the 'turnip hole' is at the centre of the Plough constellation (the Big Dipper). The dead pass through this hole and the old woman sends the pure to Wakan Tanka and the others to be reincarnated.

This reincarnation involves going back through the hole in the sky. The homesickness of the young women is the longing which, according to the Buddhist tradition, makes souls seek to reincarnate. Passing through the hole, then, is rebirth and the rope is the umbilical cord. Its manufacture from turnip fibres in the Lakota myth is connected to the round turnip representing the belly of the pregnant mother. But why, one asks, is the rope always too short? This may signify the fact that the newborn child is severed both from the spirit world and the mother when the umbilical cord is cut. It is relevant here that the umbilical cord is considered important by many Native American tribes. A Lakota mother traditionally sows it up inside a decorated pouch in the shape of either a salamander (for a boy) or a turtle (for a girl), as a talisman for the child. The Navajo bury the cord near the family home to symbolize a transition from the human mother to Mother Earth.

The differences in the returns to earth are also important. Sapana is helped by the eagle, buzzard and hawk (or in another version just by the buzzard and hawk). This points to a descent through spiritual stages, back into the material world. In addition, assistance by animal spirits is a very common theme: they often represent instinct, or aspects of the self. The young Ojibway women are brought back to earth by the desire that took them up to the sky in the first place – ironically by the physically gross wolverine. The mother of Fallen Star, however, falls to earth. This represents a common Lakota theme – that of sacrifice: her life is sacrificed for the sake of the child and for the tribe whose saviour he will become. It is also interesting that in this myth one young woman stays behind: this may indicate that the soul has some choice in whether or not to reincarnate.

15 | GLOOSKAP AND THE WATER MONSTER

This story describing one of the great creator hero's adventures is adapted from nineteenth-century sources. Versions are told by several Algonquian tribes, including the Maliseet, Micmac and Passamaquoddy. Interestingly, a similar myth is found on the North Pacific coast and across the Bering Straits in Siberia.

When Glooskap had finished creating the mountains and valleys, the rivers and forests and all the animals, he created a human village. The people in this village lived happily, with the forests and the animals providing them with everything they needed. The villagers had no need to travel far to fetch water, because they had a gushing spring that gave clear, pure water and never ran dry. But one day it did. The people going to fill their skin bags found only a slimy trickle, then nothing.

This was a disaster. The snows had recently melted and the spring ought to have been full and strong. The elders held a council and decided to send a good, reliable man north to its source to find out what had gone wrong. This man took his bow and some food wrapped in hide and set out on foot.

After several days he came to a village. He hoped that the people here would be friendly and help, but they were a strange people, with green skin and webbed hands and feet. Through their village ran a slimy, foul-smelling trickle of a stream. However, the man was very thirsty now, so he asked these people for a drink.

'We can't give you water without permission from our chief,' they told him. 'Go and ask him. You'll find him upstream.'

The man carried on until he came to a dark place where a dark green mountain cast a long shadow. It grew cold out of the sun. Then he heard a deep, croaking voice: 'Puny human, what do you want?'

The man looked around him, then realized that the voice came from the mountain towering above him – which was in fact a monster. The monster had dammed the stream and trapped all the water in a huge hole. What's more, he had fouled the water and made it poisonous for anyone else to drink. The man looked up at the monster's rough, warty skin, huge tooth-filled mouth and evil yellow eyes. But he was a brave man and he managed to speak: 'I've come to ask for water for my village. You've got it all and we need some.'

The monster blinked and boomed:

> *Do what you will, it's all one to me.*
> *If you want water, go to the sea!*

The man pleaded, but the monster just opened his huge mouth in an ugly grin, showing his sharp teeth and all the creatures he had devoured. Then he smacked his lips with a noise like a thunderclap.

At this, the man felt he had been brave enough: he turned and ran.

Back at his village, he told the people of his failed adventure and they sat miserably, at a loss for what to do. But mighty Glooskap was aware of their plight and said to himself: 'Now is the time for action.' He got himself ready for battle, painting himself blood-red – except for yellow rings round his eyes, attaching clam shells to his ears and adorning his hair with eagle feathers. He rose to his full height, twisted his face into a grimace and gave a terrifying war-cry that bounced around the mountains. Finally, he took a flinty mountain peak and sharpened it into a knife. Then he set off.

At the village of the green-skinned people he demanded water. They were afraid of him, so they gave him a little, but he threw the dirty, evil-smelling liquid away in disgust and marched on upstream.

Coming to where the Water Monster cast his huge shadow, Glooskap roared: 'Return the water to my people right away!'

The monster laughed with a sound like rocks falling, and repeated his chant.

> *Do what you will, it's all one to me.*
> *If you want water, go to the sea!*

Glooskap promptly swelled up to huge size, so that he was too big to fit into the monster's gaping mouth, and they fought a battle. Mountains were shattered, tall trees were uprooted and flung aside like twigs and the sky itself trembled. Then Glooskap hurled his knife at the monster's belly, which split open, so that a great white-water river came gushing out, filled the valley and ran on to the people's village.

Now Glooskap took the Water Monster and squeezed him hard, so that in seconds he was the size of a bullfrog. Glooskap then flung him into the swamp, where he has lived to this day.

COMMENTARY

As a culture hero with elements of the trickster about him, Glooskap resembles Raven, found in the North-West. He is like a strong, protecting father or big brother, who champions the child in the face of threat. He represents a very positive model of the father. The Water Monster is the complete opposite: a destructive, cruelly indifferent life-denying father who cuts off the source of life itself. Not only has he dammed the water, symbolically preventing the flow of the life-force through the psyche of the people, he has even fouled the water so that it is undrinkable. In other words he has debased the life-force, seeking to enlarge his own ego by keeping it all to himself.

The colossal size of the monster suggests that, like the Seneca giant Stone Coat, he may have been identified with a mountain – as indeed Glooskap himself is when he breaks off a mountain peak to use as a weapon. In another widespread version of the story, when the monster's stomach is split open, the resulting rush of water causes the great flood which is so often part of Native American creation myths.

It is interesting that the spring is dammed at its source. This, naturally, is upstream in the mountains. The man's journey on behalf of his people is therefore a spiritual one – to a higher place and to the source of the life-force. However, the fact that he fails completely, and that Glooskap has to take over rather than just helping, introduces a rather negative and fatalistic note, despite the story's happy ending.

16 | MONSTER-SLAYER AND BORN-OF-WATER VISIT THE SUN

> This story of hero-twins is part of the great Navajo origin myth. It continues from the story of Changing Woman (see Chapter 5), who is the twins' mother. The version here is adapted from an account by Washington Matthews published in 1897.

Changing Woman's twin sons, Monster-Slayer and Born-of-Water, were determined to visit their father the Sun, who had not yet been introduced to them, although he shone on them each day. They knew that it was their destiny to free the people from the monsters ravaging the land and for this they needed magical weapons that only their own father could provide.

The twins said goodbye to their mother and set out along the holy trail. Soon after dawn they saw smoke coming out of the ground a short way off. They found that this came from a house beneath the ground and that a soot-blackened ladder protruded invitingly from its smoke hole. They went and looked down and there they saw a little old woman with a round body. It was Spider Woman. She returned their gaze and addressed them: 'Welcome, grandchildren. Who are you and where are you from?'

They made no answer, but descended the ladder. When they were down inside the cool, shady room, the old woman asked them: 'Where are you going?'

'Nowhere special,' they replied together. Four times she asked, each time receiving a similar answer.

Then, with a knowing look, she asked, 'Perhaps you'd like to find your father, the Sun?'

The twins admitted to this, adding, 'If only we knew the way to his house.'

Spider Woman nodded gravely. 'The way is long and dangerous. There are many monsters living near the route you must take, and even when you arrive, your father may be far from pleased to see you. If you're still determined, you should know about the four places of danger through which you must pass: the crushing rocks, the razor-sharp reeds, the ripping cactuses and the boiling sands. However, I'll give you something to protect you from enemies.'

She gave them a charm called 'feather of the strange gods', which was a hoop with two 'life-feathers' attached – both plucked from a live eagle, as well as another life-feather. She also taught them a magic formula to calm an enemy's anger: 'Place your feet with pollen; place your hands with pollen; lay your head down with pollen. Then your feet are pollen, your hands are pollen, your body is pollen, your mind is pollen, your voice is pollen. The path is beautiful. Be calm.'

The twins thanked Spider Woman, climbed out of her smoke hole and went on their way. In time they came to the crushing rocks, the razor-sharp reeds, the ripping cactuses and the boiling sands. But with the help of Spider Woman's advice and charms, they overcame these obstacles, as well as avoiding the monsters. At last they arrived at their father's house, which stood on the water's edge.

At the threshold were two great bears, who reared up and growled threateningly, but the twins recited Spider Woman's calming words and the bears lay down peacefully. The next obstacle was a pair of serpents, who were similarly appeased. Then came fierce winds, and bolts of lightning, but even these were pacified by the soothing words.

The boys entered the large, square turquoise house of the Sun and they saw a woman sitting in the west, two fine young men in the south and two handsome young women in the north. The two young women rose silently, wrapped the twins in sky coverings of dawn, blue sky, yellow evening light and darkness and then put them up on a shelf, where they lay quietly. Soon a rattle over the door shook four times and one of the young women announced: 'Father is coming.'

In came the Sun, carrying his golden disc on his back. He took it off and hung it on a peg on the west wall, where it shook and clanged for a while until it was still. Turning angrily to the older woman, he demanded: 'Who were the two who arrived here today?'

He asked the same question four times. At length, the woman replied: 'You had better not say too much. Two young men came today looking for their father. You claim to be faithful to me while you're away – so whose sons are these?' And she indicated the two bundled-up boys.

The man took the twins down from the shelf and unwrapped them, so that the boys fell onto the floor. Then he flung them savagely at some sharp spikes of white shell on the east wall of the room. However, the boys were protected by their charms and bounced back. He flung them likewise at turquoise spikes in the south, haliotis in the west and jet in the north. Each time they bounced back unharmed.

'How I wish you were indeed my sons,' said the Sun. 'But since you're not, you can boil to death in here.' And he thrust them into an overheated sweatlodge from which steam billowed even as the flap opened for a moment. However, the winds came to the twins' assistance, creating a cool corner of the lodge for the boys.

When the boys emerged, the Sun said, 'Yes, you're my boys! Come and smoke a pipe with me.' But this was a trick: the pipe was poisoned. This time a spiny caterpillar helped the boys by giving them something to place in their mouths. At last the Sun was satisfied. 'My sons,' he said, 'I'm proud of you. What is it that you want from me?'

'We require magical weapons with which to rid the earth of monsters,' they answered.

'Sons, you've earned my trust: I'll help you in any way I can.'

So it was that the twins received magical weapons and lightning bolts, and after heroic struggles were able to free their people of the curse of the marauding monsters. It is said that only four monsters survived: age, winter, poverty and famine, which Changing Woman allowed to live on so that her people would treasure her gifts all the more.

COMMENTARY

This is a classic account of the hero's journey to seek atonement
with the father and to be granted the initiation that only the father
can provide. It is comparable with Aboriginal initiation rituals in
which the boy is taken from the mother and first challenged and
then sustained by the men of the tribe. The twins are aspects of one
hero; they are not given any distinguishing characteristics in the
story. According to an Apache account they actually have separate
fathers (see page 29), like the twins Heracles and Iphicles, and they
may embody what can be described as yin and yang aspects of one
hero. However, their essential unity is clear: they speak together,
act together and pass the same tests.

Spider Woman's help and warnings

The 'fairy godmother' of the story is Spider Woman. As in the Hopi
tribe's creator goddess of the same name, she is linked to the
spinning of life's web, rather than to entrapment. Her home beneath
the ground is a haven in the hot Arizona desert, evoking the womb
of Mother Earth. The ladder echoes the ladder by which, in
emergence myths of the Navajo and related tribes, people climb out
of the previous world into this one. (Hopis consider their
underground ceremonial chambers to embody this emergence.)

Spider Woman, for both the Navajo and the Hopis, is similar to the
helpful crones or little old men found in European folklore, whose
age may imply the accumulated wisdom of generations. In tales of
Christian saints her role is sometimes taken by the Virgin Mary. As
Joseph Campbell puts it: 'The Virgin by her intercession can win
the mercy of the Father. Spider Woman with her web can control
the movements of the Sun. The hero who has come under the
protection of the Cosmic Mother cannot be harmed.' Thus Spider
Woman protects the twins, both with her forewarning and with her
magic. The charm she gives them focuses on pollen because the
Navajo regard it as being very holy, owing to its association with
fertility and with the sun. One sees it depicted and used as a
material in their sacred dry paintings. The eagle feathers also
symbolize the sun.

The series of obstacles which the twins must pass are traps for the unwary. They are designed to prevent the passage of the would-be initiate who is spiritually or psychologically unprepared for the encounter with the divine father. Of particular interest is the pair of crushing rocks, similar to the Symplegades, through which Jason and the Argonauts must sail on their quest for the Golden Fleece. Both sets of rocks represent the illusion of duality – of good and evil, desirable and undesirable – which condemn the individual to live in a state of apprehension and to invest psychic energy in defending the ego and bolstering it by the acquisition of goods.

The House of the Sun

Having overcome the initial tests en route, the twins arrive at their father's house, which is on the shore because it is in the west, where the sun goes down. Here they must pass three sets of threshold guardians: the fearsome bears; the serpents of desire (and of the knowledge of good and evil, as in Eden); and the cosmic forces – the winds (the powers of the Four Directions) and the thunderbolts, which are linked to their father himself.

Then there is the beautiful moment when the Sun's daughters wrap the twins in 'sky coverings'. The colours represent the phases of the sun, presented in a sunwise direction: dawn, noon, evening and night. These in turn are linked to the Four Directions. This ritual of wrapping in the phases of the sun represents a further protection. It also shows that at this point the boys are still in the realm of time: they have yet to break out into eternity, which is what happens when they are initiated.

When the Sun-father comes in from his day's work, he hangs up his golden disc, demonstrating (as in his courtship of Changing Woman) that he is not exactly the sun itself, but its inner self. It is now an essential part of the hero's initiation that the father-figure is at first angry and rejecting, just as in the Pawnee story of 'The Medicine Grizzly Bear'. He is testing the twins' resolve and also granting them an initiation which consists of a dissolution of the ego, so that they emerge reborn. In fact this rebirth is emphasized by the overheated sweatlodge: sweatlodges represent the womb and the sweatlodge ceremony a rebirth (see page 52).

Finally, the twins earn the weapons that only a father, or a father-figure, can provide. Significantly they include thunderbolts, for their father is in fact a combined Sun and Sky god. Like Yahweh, Zeus and Indra, therefore, in his angry, destructive aspect he is a god of the storm; he is both sustainer and destroyer. Now they can go and do the work of heroes worldwide, destroying the unregenerate monsters of the unconscious mind.

17 | COYOTE STEALS LIGHT

This tale is loosely adapted from traditional Zuni sources. However, many of its elements are found all across North America.

One day, before the Sun and Moon had been placed in the sky to provide proper light, Coyote was out on the prairie looking for something to eat. He chased a rabbit and it escaped down its burrow. He chased a mouse and it hid under a rock. Just then he felt a wind pass over him and he glanced up – it was Eagle. Tired and hungry, Coyote sat down to rest. While he did, he noticed Eagle catch first one rabbit, then another and another. When Eagle flew close again, Coyote called out to him: 'Hey, my friend, with your talons and my talent we'd catch twice as much!'

Eagle considered this and then agreed to try a partnership. They started hunting, but after an hour or so Eagle had another three rabbits and Coyote had a beetle.

'This is hopeless,' complained Coyote. 'How can I catch anything without light! Where can we get some?'

'I think I can see some on the western horizon,' said Eagle. So they went out looking for it. After a while they came to a canyon, where Coyote slipped and slithered down the rocks, falling down holes and hurting himself.

'Try flying,' suggested Eagle.

'The problem is, I have no wings,' replied Coyote irritably.

When Coyote had struggled up the other side of the canyon, the pair continued and after a while they came to a village of sun-bleached houses. The people were conducting a spirit dance, and, seeing the power of the spirits, Coyote said, 'These people must have light!'

Sure enough they noticed after a while that the people had two boxes, one large and one small. Whenever they wanted a lot of light they opened the big one; whenever they wanted just enough light to see by, they opened the smaller one.

Coyote whispered to Eagle, 'See – they have all the light we need to hunt by. Let's steal that big box.'

Eagle suggested they just borrow it, but Coyote thought that the people would never agree to lend such a precious thing. So when the spirit dance was over and the boxes were unattended, Eagle carefully slipped the light from the small box into the larger one, grasped the large box in his strong talons and flew away, with Coyote running along and trying to keep up.

'Hey, friend – let me carry the box for a while.'

'You'll only lose it,' said Eagle.

'People will call me lazy – and it's not right that you should have to do all the work,' wheedled Coyote.

When Coyote had asked four times, Eagle felt he had better give in and let Coyote carry the box. 'But you'd better not open it yet,' warned Eagle.

They continued with Coyote now holding the box, and in a while Eagle's strong wings carried him far ahead. Coyote stopped for a rest and then thought to himself: 'I wonder what this light looks like. I'll just take a little look.'

Coyote opened the box and immediately a silver disc flew out: it was the moon. Coyote leaped after it trying to catch it, but already the moon was up in the sky and bushes and flowers began to die because it was now winter. While Coyote was busy chasing the moon, the sun, too, escaped and floated up to the sky. It floated so far away that the air grew cold and it began to snow.

Thanks to Coyote, winter had come to the earth, and it was going to take a long time for Eagle to catch the sun.

COMMENTARY

This is a typical trickster tale which has echoes of both Prometheus and Pandora's box. Coyote here demonstrates the particular qualities of early human development (both cultural and psychological) that make civilization possible and yet which cause problems: rebelliousness, a desire for improvement, the will and ability to deceive and, of course, curiosity. In this tale Coyote's trickster nature is contrasted with the more honest, heroic nature of Eagle. In a sense Coyote is identified with the moon, and Eagle with the sun.

Many myths explain how light first came into the world. In the Genesis myth the explanation is simple: God decrees it. The idea that is has to be stolen occurs in a number of Native American tales. For example there is one from the Tsimshian in the North-West in which the trickster hero Raven steals light from the sky people. For the Cherokee, a number of animals try to steal it from the other side of the world and in the end Grandmother Spider succeeds. Similar is a Slavey tale in which, during a long, dark winter, the animals steal warmth from bears which have been keeping it in a bag.

An interesting component of many of these stories is that there is a price to pay for the theft. In the case of Prometheus, there is direct and terrible punishment from Zeus. For the animals who steal warmth from the bears, the warmth causes the ice to melt, which floods the world. In the Zuni tale, the theft of the sun and moon, coupled with Coyote's foolishness, is responsible for the coming of winter. This motif may relate to the natural human assumption, stemming from childhood, that transgression leads to punishment; and conversely, if the world appears to be a punishing place, humanity must have done something to deserve it. The other interpretation is that light represents self-consciousness, for which the price paid is separation from nature. Once again, we have a version of the Fall.

18 | THE GIRL WHO WAS THE RING

This rendering of a Pawnee tale is adapted from an account recorded by ethnohistorian George Bird Grinnell, published in *Harper's Monthly*, 1901. It is based partly on a Pawnee game (versions of which were played by other Plains tribes), in which boys or young men would attempt to hurl their stick through a rolling ring of rawhide. In the story a girl is transformed into such a ring by some buffalo.

Four brothers and their sister lived in a lodge by a winding river. There was a tall cottonwood tree in front of the lodge and from this the brothers hung a rawhide strap on which the girl could swing. Whenever their supplies of dried meat were getting low, the girl would send her brothers to cut dogwood shoots for arrows. When the arrows were ready, she would get into the swing and the boys would take it in turns to push her. As the hoop of the swing moved back and forth, they would start to see dust rising on the horizon, by which they knew that the buffalo were coming.

Then all four brothers would take their bows and arrows and stand around the swing to protect their sister from the galloping buffalo. When the buffalo were close enough, the brothers would let loose a shower of arrows, shooting the heavy-headed beasts in a circle all around the swing, until the rest of the herd got frightened and ran away. So they would have plenty to eat and the dried meat would be piled high in the lodge.

One day the brothers went out to find wood for more arrows. Now Coyote had observed how the swing brought the buffalo and had seen the brothers leave. Seeing his opportunity, he visited the lodge and found the girl all alone. 'Granddaughter,' he said, 'I'm poor and hungry. I have no meat, and my children are also hungry. I told my relations that I was coming to ask you for food, but they laughed at me. They said you'd just send me away.'

The girl answered: 'Grandfather, we have plenty of meat. Take what you want. Take the fattest pieces to your children.'

Coyote began to cry and said: 'My relations were right to laugh – I don't want dried meat. I need fresh meat for my starving children. Have pity and let me put you in the swing, so as to bring the buffalo. I'll just swing you a little, to bring a few buffalo. I have a quiver full of arrows to keep you safe.'

The girl thought, then replied: 'I'm sorry, grandfather, I'll have to wait for my brothers.'

Then Coyote drew himself up and thumped his chest: 'Look at me – I'm a strong man! I can easily keep you safe from a few buffalo. I have plenty of arrows and I'm a good shot, so I need only use one for each buffalo. Please just let me swing you a little.'

At first she refused, but in the end she gave in and climbed into the swing. He began to swing her, gently at first, but then got carried away and pushed her as high as the swing would go – almost as high as the tree itself. The poor girl screamed and tried to get off, but it was too late. From all around, the buffalo were coming in great numbers. Coyote had prepared his arrows and was running around the girl, trying to kill the buffalo and keep them off her, but they crowded in on him, almost trampling him. At last he got frightened and ran into the lodge, abandoning the swinging girl.

Suddenly a young bull, leader of a big band, threw up his head as he passed under the swing and the girl disappeared. But Coyote, peeping out of the lodge door, saw on the bull's horn a ring, and then he knew that this ring was the girl. Then the bull galloped away fast with the rest of the herd.

Coyote was scared and did not know what to do. Soon he heard the girl's brothers. They had seen the dust and knew what it must mean. They hurried back, but when they reached the lodge they found Coyote just dragging himself out of a mud hole. He crawled out crying and moaning, claiming that the buffalo had trampled all over him.

'I tried to save your sister, honestly. I didn't expect so many buffalo. I thought the swing would have to go high, so that they'd see her from far off.'

The brothers sorrowfully discussed what they should do. While they were talking, Coyote stood before them and said: 'Friends, don't be downhearted. I'll get your sister back – I promise. Now I'm going on the warpath!'

He travelled on alone over the broad expanse of the prairie, wondering what he should do. At length he met a badger, who said to him: 'Brother, where are you going?'

'I'm going on the warpath,' Coyote answered boldly. 'Will you join my party?' The badger agreed and they went on. After they had gone a long way, they saw a hawk sitting on a branch of a tree by a ravine. He asked them where they were going, and they told him, inviting him to go with them. He agreed. After a time they met a fox, and asked him to join them, and he did so. Then they met a jack rabbit, who said he would go with them. They went on and at length they met a blackbird, who completed their band.

Soon after this they stopped and sat down and Coyote told them how the girl had been lost and said that he intended to get her back. Coyote told them his plan. The others listened and said that they would do whatever he told them. They were all glad to help rescue the girl.

As they stood up and got ready to start, Coyote said to the blackbird, 'Friend, you stay here until the time comes.' So the blackbird remained there where they had been talking, and the others went on. A little further on, Coyote told the hawk to stop and wait at that spot. The others went on a long way and then Coyote said to the rabbit, 'Rabbit, you stay here.' At the next place he left the fox, and last of all he left the badger. Then Coyote travelled on alone through the night and at dawn he came to the buffalo camp. He found the churned up, dusty place where the young bulls played the stick game and there he lay down.

After a time some young bulls came out and began to roll the ring and to throw their sticks at it. Coyote now pretended to be very ill. His tongue lolled out of his mouth and he staggered about and fell down and then got up again, moaning all the time. Sometimes he would get over near to where the ring was being rolled and then the young bulls would call out: 'Hey! Keep out of our way.'

After a little while Coyote pretended to be feeling better. He went over to where the young bulls were sitting and sat down with them, watching the game with the others. Every now and then two of the young bulls would argue over the game, each saying that his stick was the nearer to the ring, and sometimes this would go on for a long time. When a new dispute started, Coyote went up to the bulls and said: 'No need to quarrel – let me look. I know all about this game. I can tell which stick is nearer.' The bulls stopped talking and looked at him and then said: 'Yes, let him look. Let's hear what he says.' Then Coyote went up to the ring and looked and said, pointing: 'That stick's the nearest. That's the winner.' The bulls looked at each other and nodded their heads in agreement. Coyote decided the next dispute too, and all were satisfied.

At length two young bulls almost came to blows. Coyote came and looked and said: 'This is very close. I must look carefully, but I can't see with you all crowding round me. Why don't you all go over to that hill and sit down there while I decide?' The bulls agreed and trooped over to the hill. Then Coyote began to look. First he went to one stick and looked and then to the other. The sticks were about the same distance from the ring and for a long time it seemed that he could not decide which was nearer. He made a great show of this, and then got down on his hands and knees and squinted. At last, when his face was close to the ground, he snatched up the ring in his mouth and ran as hard as he could towards the place where he had left the badger.

The bulls all saw that he was stealing the ring and they chased after him. When the older buffalo saw the young bulls galloping, they all followed. Soon the whole herd was on the move, rushing after Coyote. He ran fast and for a long time he kept ahead of them, but close behind him the great shaggy red-brown mass of buffalo thundered along. At last Coyote began to tire. But he was getting near to where he had left the badger. Just when it seemed he could run no further and would be trampled to death, there was the badger sitting at the mouth of his hole. Coyote raced down the hill as fast as he could, and when he got to the hole he gave the ring to the badger. Just as the thundering hooves were almost on them, they both dived down into the hole with the ring.

The buffalo crowded about the hole, pawing the ground to get at Coyote and the ring, but the badger's hole ran a long way underground, and while the buffalo were digging he fled along his tunnel and came out far off and ran as hard as he could towards the brothers' lodge. Then some of the buffalo on the outside of the herd saw him and called out to the others and sounded the alarm. Then they all started running again. Each time they got close, he would stop running and dig another hole and while the buffalo were crowding around it, he would dig along underground, until he had got far beyond them and would then come to the surface and run as fast as he could.

At length the badger grew tired and felt that he could not run or dig much further. But then he emerged from the ground to see, not far off, the fox, curled up on a rock, asleep in the sun. The badger called out: 'Brother, I'm exhausted! Help me!'

The fox jumped up and ran to him and took the ring in his mouth and started running. The badger dug a deep hole and stayed there while the buffalo pounded overhead. The little fox ran fast, and for a long time he kept ahead of the buffalo.

When he was almost spent, the fox came to where the rabbit was, gave him the ring and ran into a hole. The rabbit shot off, hotly pursued by the buffalo. He ran fast on his long legs and kept ahead for a long time. When the buffalo had almost caught him, he came to where the hawk was perched.

The hawk took the ring in his claws and flew off with it glinting in the sun, while the rabbit ran off to one side and hid in the long grass. The buffalo followed the hawk, never seeming to tire. Eventually the hawk's wings began to feel like two rocks and he could only just keep over the buffalo's backs. At last he got near to where the blackbird was.

When the blackbird heard pounding hooves, he flew up on a sunflower stalk and waited. When the buffalo came to the place where he was, he flew up to the hawk and took the ring on his neck and flew along over the buffalo. The ring was heavy for so small a bird and he would alight on the backs of the buffalo and fly from one to another. The buffalo would toss their heads and try to gore him, but he kept flying from one to another, and as the buffalo in the rear were always pushing forward to get near the ring, they pushed the others ahead of them. Soon the herd passed over a hill and were rushing down to the place on the river where the brothers' lodge stood.

The brothers had been making arrows and now they had piles of them stacked up. When they saw the buffalo coming they got their bows and loosed volley after volley of arrows until they had killed a great number of buffalo and the rest fled in fear.

The blackbird had flown into the lodge with the ring and after the brothers had finished the killing, they went inside. There, sitting by the fire as they came in, was their sister, smiling sweetly as if she had never been away.

COMMENTARY

This is another trickster tale, for which much of what has already said about tricksters holds true. In this story, Coyote seems relatively well-intentioned, although his spying on the lodge and visiting only when the brothers are out of the way is suspicious. He shows characteristic wheedling persistence, as in the previous story, alternately seeking to be pitied and boasting of his manly strength and skill. Once he has prevailed upon the girl, it is his natural exuberance which makes him go too far. Then he is typically cowardly, after which he angles for sympathy once again. However, he does show equally characteristic ingenuity in laying his plan and fooling the buffalo, as well as a certain charisma in gathering together his band of followers.

The ring game

Of the game played by the buffalo, George Grinnell writes:

> Of all the games played by men among the Pawnee Indians, none was so popular as the stick game. This was an athletic contest between pairs of young men, and tested their

fleetness, their eyesight, and their skill in throwing the stick. The implements used were a ring six inches in diameter, made of buffalo rawhide, and two elaborate and highly ornamented slender sticks, one for each player. One of the two contestants rolled the ring over a smooth prepared course, and when it had been set in motion the players ran after it side by side, each one trying to throw his stick through the ring. This was not often done, but the players constantly hit the ring with their sticks and knocked it down, so that it ceased to roll. The system of counting was by points, and was somewhat complicated, but in general terms it may be said that the player whose stick lay nearest the ring gained one or more points.

The game as played by the Pawnee may not have had a special significance, though it would certainly help to train boys in accurate spear-throwing. In the context of the myth, however, it does have meaning. First, as noted in the commentary to 'Stone Boy', the four brothers living alone with their sister represent the Four Directions, while the sister is the central point at which they meet and are synthesized into a single energy. Hence she remains at home in the lodge, symbolically at the still centre of the moving universe, while the brothers are out gathering wood for arrows. It is interesting that the girl *sends* her brothers off to get wood: she has authority.

It seems that the girl alone has the magical power to swing on the hoop and bring the buffalo, and this is linked to the strange way in which she becomes the ring. Both swing-hoop and ring are symbols of what Native Americans of many tribes refer to as the 'sacred circle' or the 'circle of life'. It is also what visionary Lakota medicine man Black Elk referred to when he spoke of the 'sacred hoop of the nations'. It has solar connotations, too, which are evoked in the circle of the Lakota Sundance.

Coyote's rescue

The motif of an animal relay team is one which occurs in a number of Native American stories, such as that of Sun of Light and Man-Eagle and that of Sapana (Chapter 14). This provides an opportunity for repetition (with some variation) which is a popular feature in Native American narrative. However, it also carries a social message: every member of the group has a particular skill to offer; if individuals work as a team they can achieve more than they can working alone.

The motif also honours the unique talents of each member of the team. This team motif continues to occur frequently in popular culture, as in the films *The Seven Samurai* and *The Magnificent Seven*, and if we count Coyote and his band they do indeed add up to seven. One explanation for the mythical occurrences is that the seven relate to the Sun, Moon and five planets visible to the naked eye, to each of which many peoples have attributed individual powers and attributes.

Hopi rock drawing of Coyote

19 | THE SEVERED HEAD

The fact that this Cheyenne story is initially set by a lake suggests an origin prior to the tribe's migration to the Plains in the eighteenth century, while the feature of the prickly pears may have entered the tale after the tribe had been forcibly relocated in Oklahoma in the late nineteenth century. The version here is adapted from a 1903 account by George Bird Grinnell.

A small family lived on the shores of a great lake, from which they took all their water. The father was never very successful in his hunting, so the family were often hungry. Every day he went out with his bow, but first he would take steps to protect his wife from harm: she would have to remove her dress while he applied red medicine paint to the whole of her body. After he left, she would always leave the children to play in the lodge and take her skin bags down to the lakeside to fetch water.

Now the man could not help but notice a strange fact. Every evening when he returned, there was not one trace of red paint left on his wife, and her hair was unbraided and hung long and loose over her shoulders. So one day he quietly asked his son and daughter, 'Where does your mother go while I'm gone? I paint her every day, but when I return there's no sign of it.'

'She always goes to fetch water, but it seems to take her most of the day,' said the girl.

The man thought about this. The next day he painted his wife as usual, but then he went quickly down to the lake, dug a hole in the sand and hid in it. He had been there only a short time when his wife appeared with her skin bags. She stepped out of her dress, unbraided her hair and let it fall and then called out across the rippling water, 'I'm here!'

At this, the water bubbled and swirled and a shape emerged, green and dripping. It was a spirit man. Streaming with water, he crawled out onto the shore, wrapped himself around the woman, and proceeded to lick off every trace of red paint from he body.

Furious at this sight, the husband sprang out of his hiding place and attacked the water spirit with his hunting knife. He chopped its slippery green body up into pieces, which crept and crawled back into the water. Then he turned on his wife in a jealous rage and stabbed her, then cut off her head and limbs and flung these into the water, shouting: 'Here's your wife – she's yours!' Then he sliced open his wife's body and removed one side of her ribs, with the flesh on them.

Calmer now, but still full of bitter thoughts, he washed the blood from his hands and then took his wife's flesh back to the lodge. The children came out, surprised to see him back so soon. He seemed to have been lucky in his hunting for once.

'Look, children, I've killed a deer. We'll eat well today! Where's your mother?'

'She went to fetch water,' said the boy.

'Well, then, get a pot of water on the fire and we'll cook up some meat ourselves.'

Then he boiled up the ribs and flesh and gave the children their meal. They ate hungrily, but the boy, who was the younger child, was puzzled. 'This tastes like our mother,' he said.

'Don't be silly,' said his sister. 'This is venison. We'll save some for mother to eat when she gets home with the water.'

Their father then gathered up his things, pretending that he was going out hunting again. But in fact he had resolved to abandon the children and go in search of his tribe.

After the father had gone, the children were left alone as usual. The girl was starting to decorate some moccasins with coloured porcupine quills, when they heard a voice: 'My children can't love me very much – they've eaten me!'

The children were scared, but the boy looked out of the door to see whose voice it was. Then he said in a small voice, 'It's – our mother's head.'

'Quick,' said the girl. 'Shut the door.' She snatched up her moccasins, her quills and her root digger. Meanwhile the head was repeatedly banging at the door to be let in. Then the children went to the door and stood to one side. When the girl opened it wide, the head came rolling in. And while it was rolling across the floor, the children ran outside, shut the door behind them and fled, with their mother's voice fading behind them.

When the boy pleaded that he could go no further, they stopped on a hill and looked back. Off in the distance they could see their mother's head bouncing along towards them. They ran on, but after a while they could see that the head was gaining on them and the boy was stumbling and terrified.

The girl found that she was thinking about when she was little, and how the prickly pears were sometimes so high and thick that she couldn't get through them. As this thought came to her, she took a handful of her quills – the yellow ones – and scattered them behind her. At once a broad forest of prickly pear cactuses grew up.

This held the head up for a long time, and by the time it managed to find a way through the obstacle, the children were far ahead. Again, however, they looked back and saw that it was getting closer. The girl now found herself thinking about how thick the spiny bullberry bushes used to grow, and she turned and scattered a handful of white quills on the ground. At once a thick patch of the bushes sprang up, and when the head reached them, once again it was held up as it tried to find a way through the spikes.

The children ran on and again saw the head catching up. This time the girl thought about thorny rose bushes and so she cast a handful of red quills behind her, which quickly turned into a dense thicket of rose bushes. This checked the head's relentless progress as before, but eventually it struggled through and continued the pursuit.

Now the two children stopped, gasping, their chests feeling as if they would burst. The girl remembered that when she was small she would often come across little ravines that she was unable to cross. So she took out her root-digging stick and scratched a thin furrow in the dry soil behind them. Quickly this furrow turned into a ditch and then a deep ravine with steep sides and a trickle of a stream in the bottom.

The boy was about to start running on, but the girl said: 'We'll stay here. This is where I'll kill our mother.'

In a few minutes the head rolled up to the ravine and came to a halt on its brink. 'My daughter,' it called, 'lay your digging-stick across the ravine for me so that I can cross.' The boy tried to stop her doing it, but despite this the girl managed to lay her stick across the ravine, and the head began to cross. But when it was half-way, the girl up-ended the stick and the head plunged into the ravine. At this, the earth heaved and swallowed it up for good.

Walking slowly on, they saw smoke rising from lodges, and when they came closer saw that it was their tribe's camp. When they came into the village, they shyly crouched down by a tipi and listened. Then they heard a man's voice – their father's! But he was telling the people about how his two monstrous children had killed and eaten their own mother. The children wondered if they should sneak away quietly, but how would they survive? So they went into the camp, hoping for the best. However, when people spotted them and realized who they were, the children were captured and tied up. The next day the people moved camp and the children were abandoned once more.

They began to despair. But in the camp there was an old dog, a bitch with pups. She had taken pity on the children and stolen a knife, an awl and some sinew for them, thinking that these would be useful. Then when the people had gone, she went to the children and started to untie the girl. The toothless old dog took a long time over this, but eventually the girl was free and could untie her brother. Then the children wandered about the deserted camp looking for old moccasins to wear, because theirs had been worn out in the chase.

They found moccasins, but their troubles were not yet over. There was no food and when a wolf came towards them, they thought their end had come. Strangely, however, when the girl looked at the wolf, it dropped down dead. Now they had food. The children used the stolen knife to butcher the wolf, made a fire, then cooked and ate it. From the wolfskin they made a bed for the dog and her pups. Meanwhile the tribe, a few miles away, were starving.

After the last scrap of wolf meat was gone, the children became hungry again. A deer wandered close to them and they wished they had some means of killing it. But when the girl stared at it, it fell dead. They ate well now and fed the liver to the old dog.

The time came when the deer was all eaten and the children wondered where their next meal was coming from. Then a big elk wandered close and the girl looked at it and it died. They ate and again fed the dog, then stretched the elk hide to make a good shelter. They also used the awl and sinews to mend their moccasins. Then when a buffalo came by and the girl looked at it with the same deadly result, they were able to eat really well, and make an even better shelter.

One night it snowed, and as the girl went to bed, she said, 'I wish we had a proper lodge over there, with beds, and that my brother were a young man able to hunt the buffalo with a bow and arrows.' In the morning they awoke and looked outside. To the amazement of both children, there was a fine new lodge with its flap open to welcome them. They went to it and when the boy stepped inside, he immediately became a young man. Now he was able to hunt the buffalo – and he was a better hunter than his father had ever been.

Things were going well for the girl and her brother now, but one night the girl made another wish. She wished that they had two bears to help them get revenge on their father for the terrible way in which he had treated them. In the morning, there were two big grizzlies sitting outside the lodge.

'Bears, you must be hungry,' said girl. 'Come and eat.' And she fed them well. Then she took another piece of good meat and called to a raven perched nearby. 'Raven, please help me. Take this meat to my tribe. Fly around so that they can see the meat. Drop it in their midst. When they ask where it came from, tell them that we have plenty of meat here piled up on our racks.'

The raven did as she asked and was rewarded. As for the people, when they thought about the prospect of full bellies, they quickly decided to move to where the girl and her brother lived. They pulled down their lodges, hardly bothering to pack up properly, and set out as soon as they could. When they reached the camp of the girl and her brother, the people saw that there was indeed a huge supply of meat – enough for all of them. The girl invited them to eat and they pushed and jostled to get to the meat, throw it in their mouths and take some away. The girl sent a message to her father to come later, so that he would not have to be pushed about in the crowd, but would be able to eat at his leisure.

Then she spoke to the two bears: 'I have a special meal for you, but you'll have to wait for it. When the man who comes last has eaten and I give you the word, you can eat him.'

The bears looked forward to this and waited in the bushes. Then when the last of the people had eaten, the girl sent for her father. He arrived, looking sheepish. 'At last I've found you my dear children,' he said. 'I'm glad to see you've done so well for yourselves.'

He ate greedily and made up a package of meat to take away with him. Then, as he left the lodge, the girl called out to the bears: 'Dinner time!'

The bears rushed out grunting and roaring and knocked down the terrified man. 'Call off these animals!' he shouted. But it was no use – the bears tore him to pieces. When they had eaten well, the bears threw the remains in a streambed and no one ever knew what had happened to the father.

From that day on bears have eaten human flesh when they could get it. As for the girl and her brother, they lived happily and prospered.

COMMENTARY

This story falls into two distinct halves, the second beginning after the children dispatch their mother's head. One wonders if two separate stories have been combined, although the two halves are unified by the children's revenge on their father. The tale overall has many of the vivid ingredients that enliven myths worldwide: infidelity, jealous rage, a hair-raising pursuit and violent revenge.

The abandoned children motif

Like many Native American stories, the focus is on children who are mistreated and either orphaned or abandoned. Stith Thompson (*The Folktale*) identifies a category of tale, spread across the whole of North America, which he calls 'The deserted children'. In this, a group of children are abandoned by a tribe unable to support them. They go to an old woman, who kills all but two – a girl and her brother. The pair flee, pursued by the old woman, who is tricked by magical objects which the girl leaves behind. After being carried over a river by a water monster, the children find their tribe, but are rejected again. A friendly animal helps them, both children perform magical feats by their glance (including killing animals), and the starving tribe are forced to beg the children for food. The similarities are obvious, and the story may have social origins in the actual abandonment of children in difficult times. There are even some similarities with European folktales, such as 'Hansel and Gretel'.

Repressed urges

Given the unpleasant character of the husband, the fact that he paints his wife red every day suggests jealous suspicion rather than real concern, so that when he catches her with the water spirit it is no more than he deserves. In fact a water spirit that crawls out of the lake strongly suggests a creature of the unconscious, and it may represent the man's jealous imaginings. Certainly it gives him an excuse to kill his wife.

In most cultures cannibalism is a major taboo. This may be why myths and folktales contain many instances of people being tricked into it. In Greek myth, for example, Tantalus serves the gods a stew made of his own son. Another father, Thyestes, is tricked into eating his own murdered children. A Freudian or Kleinian interpretation of the Cheyenne tale might point to repressed infantile urges to devour or destroy the mother. From this viewpoint, the tale enacts, and in part satisfies, this urge. The fact that the children are tricked makes their breaking of the taboo more acceptable.

The pursuit

Societies all over the world have had cults of the head. The ancient
Celts thought of the head as having great power, and would often
preserve it after death. The image of the head pursuing the children
is frightening, although it is never made clear what it is going to do
to them if it ever catches up! The delayed pursuit is a common
motif in myth and folktale, and one still found in popular culture.
Typically the fugitives throw behind them objects that will slow
down their pursuer. One example (also involving dismemberment)
is that of Jason and Medea, who leave behind a trail of body parts
from the brother whom Medea has murdered, so that her pursuing
father will have to stop and bury them.

Joseph Campbell interprets this 'delayed pursuit' motif as evidence
of the ego's attempts to avoid a confrontation with the divine for
which it is unready. However, it may be that the head in this story
represents the supernatural rather than the divine. There may be
more spiritual virtue in the powers which the girl summons, which
seem to be those of the Four Directions, and which create the four
obstacles. When the girl finally buries the mother's head, this
seems to be more about burying her memory than avoiding
divinity. The ravine which opens up is a version of the 'great
divide' between life and death, which is a feature of the story which
follows. The girl refuses to place a bridge across it for her mother.

The helpful animals

The old dog is an archetypal animal helper and the three tools that
she provides are also repeated in other stories. Significantly, the
children look after the dog, repaying her kindness to them, and so
they are rewarded in turn. The girl's ability to kill game with a
glance may refer to shamanistic skills or just wishful thinking.
However, it is interesting that once again we have a group of four,
perhaps linked to the Directions, with the buffalo in the north
coming last. The suggestion of shamanistic abilities gets stronger
as the story continues, with the girl able to call on the raven and the
bears for help.

A typical Native American twist to the tale is contained in the explanatory device at the end: bears have eaten human flesh ever since. This explanation is clearly not the main purpose of the story, but it does have the virtue of providing a sense of conclusion that connects the tale to the present day.

20 | THE LOVING HUSBAND

This Zuni myth is one of a number of traditional Native American tales which echo the Greek myth of Orpheus and Eurydice.

There was a young man who married a woman whom he loved very much. The couple were happy, but all too soon the woman became ill and died. The husband was distraught and wandered the desert calling her name for days. Then, resolving to call up her spirit, he made prayer sticks, sprinkled magical pollen and coloured an eagle's feather red. Just as the moon was rising, full and golden in the east, a small wind blew and his wife's spirit came to him.

'Don't be sad,' she said, comfortingly. 'I'm going to the spirit world.'

'Then I'll go with you,' said the young man desperately.

The woman did her best to persuade him to carry on living in this world, and even to take a new wife, but he would not listen. At length, she sighed like the soft desert breeze and told him: 'If you're determined to follow me, there is a way. We must set off at dawn, but first you must tie the eagle feather in my hair so that you can see me when I become invisible in the daylight.'

Relieved that there was now hope, the young man did as she said. Then he spent the rest of the night praying with her, while the coyotes howled around them and the owl's swift moon shadow passed silently over the desert.

In the pale pre-dawn light the woman began to fade from view. Soon she disappeared completely, but the eagle feather was still visible, bobbing along a little way ahead of the man as he hastened westwards across the desert. The red feather floated along evenly above even the most rugged terrain. While the man clambered over rocks and crumbling dry earth, tiring rapidly as the sun rose high, the feather kept its steady pace.

The day wore on and then night fell. The wife appeared to him now in dreams, encouraging him to carry on. At daybreak as she faded from him, he forced himself back on the trail, following the feather for hour after hour.

For days they continued in this way. The path became harder, the man more exhausted. He hardly ate or drank and he could not even be sure anymore that the feather was really there. Then again the dreams came, sometimes now even in the dazzling glare of the sun, and he was reassured.

Then one morning he pulled up short, dry earth scattering before him. He was standing on the brink of a deep canyon. Its sides were sheer and there seemed to be no path down to its distant floor or up the other side. 'Wife, wait!' the man called, his words faintly issuing from a parched mouth. But the feather continued across the canyon without him. Terrified of losing his wife after coming so far, the man searched for a way down and began to climb down the slightest of cracks, his fingers clinging to whatever protuberances in the rock he could find. As he climbed, rocks fell from beneath his feet and plunged far into the bottom of the canyon.

Too far down to think about turning back, he found himself clinging with straining fingers to a tiny ledge, his feet hardly supported. Then he heard a chattering sound.

'You've got yourself into a mess here. You're going to need my help!' A tiny striped squirrel had appeared from nowhere and was perched on the ledge beside him. It reached into its cheek pouch and produced a small seed, which it tucked into a crack in the rock just big enough to hold it. In moments the seed sprouted a little green shoot, which quickly became a twining stalk and then a strong branch that reached out right across the canyon to the other side.

'What are you waiting for!' said the squirrel and disappeared.

The man gratefully reached for the branch and clambered on. Awkwardly, because of his tiredness, he pulled himself across the canyon. His heart lifted when he found the feather waiting for him on the other side, just bobbing gently on the air.

Towards evening, however, the feather led him to a broad, dark lake. The rocky ground sloped steeply down to it, and it looked very deep. A chill hung on the air here. The feather came to the lake's edge and then plunged in and was gone. The man sat and lost himself to desolation. As the sun was going down, he heard a bird calling. Then he heard the soft sound of wings and turned to see an owl beside him.

'I know the reason for your sorrow,' said the owl. 'Follow me and you'll live to see your wife again.'

The owl led the way to a mountain cave and invited the young man into a chamber full of owl people. They welcomed him and fed him his first meal for days, and he rested. Then the owl man produced a skin bag and said: 'This medicine will send you to sleep. When you wake, follow the Morning Star to the middle anthill and there you'll find your wife. When dawn comes, she'll be alive again and yours once more. But be warned: if you touch her in any way before you arrive safely in your village, all will be lost.'

The owl man then blew sleep medicine from the bag into the face of the young man, who immediately fell deeply asleep. Then the owl people took him to the dark lake and laid him down on its edge. Then with the help of prayer sticks they were able to dive to the land of the dead at the bottom of the lake. Here they administered more of the sleep medicine to the spirits who guard the souls of the dead and so were able to take the man's wife back to the lakeshore.

When the man awoke, he saw the Morning Star shining brightly in the west. He walked towards the middle anthill and was overjoyed to find his own dear wife sleeping there. Remembering the owl's instructions, he resisted the urge to touch her and spoke her name instead. She awoke and smiled at him, 'Your love must be very strong,' she said. 'Now let's go home.'

They set off and the way seemed much easier for the man now, with his wife beside him. After three days travelling eastwards, they could see their village off in the distance. Thinking that their lasting happiness was ensured, the wife said, 'I'm so tired, husband. And I'll have to greet everyone in the village and explain where I've been. Let me sleep a little to be refreshed for our return.'

The wife lay down and slept, and the man watched over her. After a while, however, she moved in her sleep and a strand of hair fell across her face. She looked so pretty that the man entirely forgot the owl man's warning. Softly, so as not to wake her, he reached across and stroked the hair from her face.

That moment the wife awoke and started back in horror. Then she became sad. 'You loved me so much,' she said, 'but still not enough.' At that she began to fade, and in moments she was lost to her husband for ever.

COMMENTARY

Myths and folktales in which a hero travels to the land of the dead in an attempt to fetch back a loved one are found all over the world. This is, perhaps, a natural enough theme: the bereaved feel that they would do anything to bring the loved one back, even go to the land of the dead. Joseph Campbell sees the theme as a reassuring one, in that it at least offers the hope of overcoming death, even if the expedition usually fails. The eagle feather that the young man follows represents both the sun and spirit itself, but it could also be taken to represent hope. Indeed there are similar Native American tales in which the hero is successful. In one Blackfoot tale not only does the husband secure his wife, he also receives a sacred pipe (the 'Worm Pipe').

The path to the land of the dead is usually seen as arduous, for the living if not for the dead themselves. The young man is making a journey of the spirit and the desert aptly represents the testing that he undergoes. Except that the goal is a different one, the journey is not unlike that of Long Arrow (Chapter 11), who goes to look for elk dogs; it also recalls Arrow Boy's visit to the mountain cave (Chapter 7). All three heroes go on long journeys which eventually lead into the mountains, which are of course related to the realm of spirit. The Zuni story contains both the mountain cave found in Arrow Boy's story, and the mountain lake as portal to another world, found in Long Arrow's.

The chasm and the cave

The first great obstacle faced by the Zuni husband is the sheer-sided canyon. The yawning chasm or 'great divide' is often used mythically as a metaphor for whatever divides life from death. Its purpose is to prevent any passage between the two worlds. Here the husband is almost lost, but is rescued by the timely assistance of a magical animal helper of the kind so often found in Native American stories. The striped squirrel is sometimes the only obvious sign of life in the American desert and its quick movements convey a keen sense of the life-force. The seed that this squirrel causes to sprout in a crack in the rock is of course a metaphor for this force. The bridge thus formed is an extension of this life-force, so strong that it can carry the young man over onto the other side – almost to the land of the dead.

The owl-man is another spirit helper. For many tribes the owl is unlucky, but the Zuni often see owls in this helpful guise or as embodying the spirits of respected departed elders. The owl cave, as in the story of Arrow Boy, is an example of access to the spirit world by a descent into the unconscious, as well as into Mother Earth. It is interesting that the owl does not enable the husband to dive into the lake and reach the land of the dead himself. (In this respect he is unlike Orpheus.) Instead he sends him to sleep, which is another way of enabling the man to contact the spirit world.

Awakening and loss

When the man awakes he sees the planet Venus, which in its guise as the Morning Star is regarded by the Zuni as an important spirit. He finds his wife and they set off. As in the Orpheus myth, the fatal error occurs when the couple are almost safe. It may be that the young man's sexual desire is the key element here, but this is not necessarily the case, and it is not the case with Orpheus. It could be that the wife has to return fully to the relatively base human condition before it is safe to touch her. It seems more likely, however, that the wife's return to the land of the dead was always inevitable and that the husband's error is simply a means of ensuring it. The Zuni myth may ultimately be about the husband learning the hard lesson that death cannot be overcome.

CONCLUSION

It should by now be apparent that the Native American oral tradition differs in many ways from the mythical canon generally taken as a standard by readers from the European cultural tradition – that of the Greeks. Many Greek myths are exclusively about the gods, and there are no myths in which the gods do not play a major role in directing human affairs. This is also true of many other myth systems, such as the Norse and Hindu.

Some Native American myths do fit this classical model. The elaborate creation myths of the Hopi and Navajo revolve around gods and spirits and explore the first principles of existence. There is a pantheon of gods, which in the Navajo case focuses on the 'holy family' of the Sun, Changing Woman and the Hero-Twins. The Lakota, too, identify a pantheon, as shown in Chapter 2, although its gods rarely occur outside the creation myth. However, taken overall there are relatively few Native American myths involving gods.

Neither are there many examples of 'euhemerization' – the process, common in the Celtic tradition, by which mythical deities are gradually cloaked in human characteristics. This happens to a limited extent in Navajo myths, but figures such as Changing Woman are still clearly divine rather than human.

Another difference between Native American myths and the familiar classical model is that many classical myths appear to have developed from legends; that is, they are based on historical characters and events. Heroes such as Theseus and Heracles crop up in a number of episodes and have many great deeds ascribed to them. With Native American myths this is rarely the case, although we have seen some instances of key events in tribal history being mythologized, as in 'Long Arrow and the Elk Dogs' (Chapter 11).

Yet despite the differences, Native American myths contain many themes found all over the world. The creation myths describe light being born out of darkness, like the earliest Greek myths or the Genesis myth. The successive worlds of the emergence myths, which represent the evolution of human consciousness, are paralleled by the successive generations of gods in Greek and Norse myths; and the many flood myths are similar to those of the Hebrews, Mesopotamians and Chinese.

Another strong similarity is found in those Native American myths that do contain deities or magical figures. White Buffalo Woman strongly resembles the virgin goddess of wisdom Pallas Athene; Changing Woman compares with Demeter; and the tiny hero of the Seneca tale 'The Powerful Boy' shows a similarly precocious and disruptive energy to that of the infant Hermes. Glooskap's mastery of the water-withholding monster is on a par with Thor's battle with the giant serpent of Midgard or the Babylonian hero Marduk's slaying of the monster Tiamat.

Perhaps the strongest similarities, however, are found in the archetypal hero myth. The young man leaves his mother, goes in search of his father, is tested by him (often being sent on a quest), overcomes the father's anger and rejection and receives his blessing, frequently bringing back a boon for his people. The Navajo Twins go in search of their father the Sun, are tested and nearly killed by him and then win his love; Medicine Bear undergoes a similar testing by a father-figure grizzly bear. Both these stories compare with that of Theseus, who passes his father's test by removing a sword and sandals from under a rock, goes to Athens to find him, is sent on a dangerous quest and then nearly poisoned by him, and finally wins his love.

These heroes are often helped to achieve a goal that benefits their people. Arrow Boy is guided to the underwater spirit world by the beautiful boy who turns into a kingfisher. He is tested by a father-figure and given the gift of horses; the Navajo Twins are helped through the desert by Spider Woman. Similarly, Theseus is given a ball of thread by Ariadne, which enables him to find his way out of the labyrinth after he has killed the Minotaur and saved the lives of the Athenian youths.

There is also the special case of the 'Orphic' hero, who attempts to bring back a loved one from the dead, but fails. The story of the Zuni husband relates not only to Orpheus, but more widely to the Sumerian Inanna's descent into the Underworld and the Norse Hermod's failed expedition to Hel to plead for the life of Balder.

Finally, as noted in Chapter 1, the hero is related to the trickster. The North American tricksters Coyote, Iktome and Raven are more ambiguous than the Norse Loki, the Celtic Bricriu or the West African Edshu, often displaying heroic aspects to their character. Nevertheless the basic characteristics are broadly the same, and all these tricksters are essentially divine.

Native American stories, then, whether regarded as myths or folktales, contain all the essential ingredients of myths worldwide, albeit in a form very much influenced by the varied tribal societies in which they have evolved. Given the geographical isolation of North America from the rest of the world until modern times, this fact argues persuasively for a common origin for these motifs in the pool of the collective unconscious.

Zuni pottery

BIBLIOGRAPHY

Books

Black Elk, Charlotte, *Sioux Nation Black Hills Act: Hearing Before the Senate Select Committee on Indian Affairs*, United States Senate 99th Congress Second Session on S. 1453, 16 July 1986, Washington, DC: US Govt Printing Office, 1986, p. 204

Boaz, Frazer, *The Way of Myth: Talking with Joseph Campbell*, Shambhala, 1994

Brown, Joseph Epes (ed.), *The Sacred Pipe*, Penguin, Harmondsworth, 1972

Campbell, Joseph, *The Hero with a Thousand Faces*, Fontana, 1993

Debo, Angie, *A History of the Indians of the United States*, Pimlico, London, 1995

Erdoes, R. and Ortiz, A., *American Indian Myths and Legends*, Pimlico 1997

Goodman, Ronald, *Lakota Star Knowledge*, Sinte Gleska University, Rosebud, 1992

Grimes, Richard S., 'Modern Spartans on the Great Plains: the ascent of the Cheyenne Dog Soldiers, 1838–1869', *Journal of the Indian Wars*, vol. 1, 4 (available on web)

Grinnell, George Bird, *Pawnee Hero Stories and Folk-Tales*, University of Nebraska Press, 1961

– *Blackfoot Lodge Tales: The Story of a Prairie People*, University of Nebraska Press, 1962

– *By Cheyenne Campfires*, University of Nebraska Press, 1971

– *The Punishment of the Stingy and Other Indian Stories*, University of Nebraska Press, 1982

Hand, Floyd Looks for Buffalo, *Learning Journey on the Red Road*, Learning Journey Communications, Toronto, 1998

Josephy, Alvin M., *The Indian Heritage of America*, Penguin, Harmondsworth, 1975

Jung, Carl (ed.), *Man and His Symbols*, Arkana, 1964

Lame Deer and Erdoes, R, *Lame Deer, Seeker of Visions*, Simon & Schuster, 1972

Miller, Lee, *From the Heart*, Pimlico, London, 1997

Neihardt, John G., *Black Elk Speaks*, Abacus, London, 1974

Pritchard, Evan T., *No Word for Time,* Council Oak Books, Tulsa, 1997

Sandner, Carl, *Navajo Symbols of Healing*, Healing Arts Press, Vermont, 1979

Sherman, Josepha, *Indian Tribes of North America*, Richard Todd, 1996

Stolzman, Fr. William (First Eagle), *How to Take Part in Lakota Ceremonies,* Tipi Press, Chamberlain, 1995

Thompson, *The Folktale*, University of California Press, 1946

Walker, James R., *Lakota Belief and Ritual*, University of Nebraska, Lincoln, 1991

Waters, Frank, *The Book of the Hopi*, Ballantine Books, New York, 1969

Wyman, Leland C., *Blessingway*, University of Arizona Press, 1970

Zimmerman, Larry J., *Native North America*, Macmillan, London, 1996

Websites

The following is a selection of Websites that have proved useful.

Keeler, F. *Black Hills and Stone Boy: A New Interpretation?* (Parts I and II), http://nativenet.uthscsa.edu/arc

Navajo Religion, http://www.newage.com.au/panthology/navajo.html

Strom, Karen M., *Voyage to Another Universe*, http://www.hanksville. org/voyage/index.html

http://www.angelfire.com/ca/Indian/stories.html

http://angelfire.com/tx2/ecc/caddo.html

http://members.tripod.com/lafitte-r/turtle.html

http://www.indians.org/welker/heron.htm

http://www.zicahota.com.maxpages

INDEX

ty TEACH YOURSELF

GREEK MYTHS

Steve Eddy and Claire Hamilton

Myths are symbolic stories that have evolved through oral tradition, and they have guided and inspired us for many years. Follow these lively retellings of popular and significant Greek myths and discover how to unlock their hidden meanings so that they can be better understood.

- Explore and enjoy the subtle truths these tales have to offer.
- Discover more about the heritage of Greek mythology.
- Bring these ancient myths to life by discovering how to interpret them.
- Place Greek myths in a cultural and global context.

Steve Eddy is a former English teacher and author of several books on esoteric subjects. Claire Hamilton is a writer, performer and Celtic harpist. She has explored myths in all these capacities and has an MA in The Bardic Tradition in Ireland.

CELTIC MYTHS

Steve Eddy and Claire Hamilton

Myths are symbolic stories that have evolved through oral tradition, and they have guided and inspired us for many years. Follow these lively retellings of popular and significant Celtic myths and discover how to unlock their hidden meanings so that they can be better understood.

■ Explore and enjoy the subtle truths these tales have to offer.
■ Discover more about the heritage of Celtic mythology.
■ Bring these ancient myths to life by discovering how to interpret them.
■ Place Celtic myths in a cultural and global context.

Steve Eddy is a former English teacher and author of several books on esoteric subjects. Claire Hamilton is a writer, performer and Celtic harpist. She has explored myths in all these capacities and has an MA in The Bardic Tradition in Ireland.

CHINESE MYTHS

Te Lin

Myths are symbolic stories that have evolved through oral tradition, and they have guided and inspired us for many years. Follow these lively retellings of popular and significant Chinese myths and discover how to unlock their hidden meanings so that they can be better understood.

- Explore and enjoy the subtle truths these tales have to offer.
- Examine the mythical heritage of China.
- Bring these ancient myths to life by discovering how to interpret them.
- Explore Chinese mythological symbolism.

Te Lin has an extensive background in the study and application of myth. She is a trained counsellor and has maintained a private counselling practice for ten years, using mythical themes, where appropriate, to expand understanding. She has written extensively on myths and related matters.